THE GOOD OFFICE

THE GOOD OFFICE

GREEN DESIGN ON THE CUTTING EDGE

JOHN RIORDAN, LEED AP AND KRISTEN BECKER, LEED AP

COLLINS DESIGN
An Imprint of HarperCollinsPublishers

SPECIAL THANKS TO: Saul Becker, Gwen Shlichta, Dr. Michael Welton, Dotty and Kelly Riordan, James Trulove, our families, friends, publisher, and the design professional, clients, and users all of whom directly participated in the making of the content of this book. We are indebted to all of you. This book would not have been possible without your vision, execution, and help.

HarperCollins books may be purchased for educational, business, or sales promotional use. For information, please write: Special Markets Department, HarperCollins*Publishers*, 10 East 53rd Street, New York, NY 10022.

First published in 2008 by:
Collins Design
An Imprint of HarperCollins*Publishers*
10 East 53rd Street
New York, NY 10022
Tel: (212) 207-7000
Fax: (212) 207-7654
collinsdesign@harpercollins.com
www.harpercollins.com

Distributed throughout the world by:
HarperCollins*Publishers*
10 East 53rd Street
New York, NY 10022
Fax: (212) 207-7654

Packaged by:
Grayson Publishing, LLC
James G. Trulove, Publisher
1250 28th Street NW
Washington, DC 20007
(202) 337-1380
jtrulove@aol.com

Designed by: Agnieszka Stachowicz

Library of Congress Control Number: 2007941134
ISBN: 978-0-06-153789-9

Printed in China
First printing, 2008

KEY	
■	NEW CONSTRUCTION
■	ADAPTIVE REUSE
■	CERTIFICATION (LEED OR BREEAM)
■	LAND CONSERVATION

CONTENTS

FOREWORD

Our built environments affect us profoundly. We spend many more waking hours indoors in the workplace than we do outdoors. Poor air quality, limited access to natural daylight and exposure to off-gassing toxic building materials are only a few elements in traditional office environments that have contributed to absenteeism and illness. More employers recognize the importance of investing in the health and well-being of their employees and the environment by building green.

The Good Office features 25 offices from seven countries and nine states that demonstrate innovative ways to integrate sustainable principles into the design of the workplace. This book has identified four notable categories that organize the projects: New Construction, Adaptive Reuse, Land Conservation and Certification. Each category shows how embedding sustainable building principles into a design take many forms and approaches.

The "New Construction" projects have an opportunity to integrate sustainable strategies into all areas of the design from the ground up. A key to the success of ground up projects such as the Genzyme Center is that architect, contractor and consultants were brought together early on to collectively develop a sustainable building strategy to lower running, maintenance and energy costs.

The "Adaptive Reuse" category includes projects that breathe new life into an existing neglected structure that might have otherwise been demolished. These projects include the Moore Foundation building, which found a new home in a 19th Century military structure and the Sedgwick Rd office that reused an old machinery building as the home for their advertising agency in Seattle. The adaptive reuse projects successfully demonstrate that reusing a building can be a first step in building sustainably.

LEFT: Sedgwick Rd. Photo: Tim Bies.

The "Land Conservation" projects are built on environmentally sensitive, abandoned, or underused industrial sites and, these factors make, redevelopment a more complex undertaking. Projects such as the Save the Bay Foundation chose to restore a damaged industrial site. The Chesapeake Bay Foundation takes into consideration the sensitivity of the Chesapeake Bay ecosystem and extend their commitment to the environment beyond the boundaries of the building.

The "Certified" category denotes whether the given projects have sought certification through a third-party certification program such as the United States Green Building Council's LEED (The Leadership in Energy and Environmental Design) program or BREEAM (Building Research Establishment Environmental Assessment Method). An office does not need to be certified to be green, but the checklists that these programs provide can be used as a guideline for building green. Some of the projects fall into multiple categories which underscores how sustainable design methodologies can be employed in all aspects of the design and building process. The projects as a whole transform our idea of what makes an office sustainable. These offices are more than just a place you work, they are innovative and beautiful work environments that invite creativity and promote healthier living.

LEFT: Save the Bay Foundation. Photo: Ruggero Vanni.

Chesapeake Bay Foundation

PHILIP MERRILL ENVIRONMENTAL CENTER

ARCHITECT: Smith Group

AREA: 32,000 Square Feet

LOCATION: Annapolis, Maryland

PHOTOGRAPHER: Prakash Patel

The new headquarters for the largest nonprofit regional environmental organization in the United States is an icon for sustainability. Winner of numerous awards for its innovative and sustainable design concepts, this foundation office building has been hailed by environmentalists and business leaders alike. The large facility, which is set lightly upon the sensitive bay ecosystem, earned the first top LEED rating of Platinum in the nation from the United States Green Building Council.

All design decisions, from the siting and orientation of the building to the selection of even the smallest building materials, examined the impact on the habitats within the 64,000-square-mile watershed. Environmentally innovative building systems and strategies were designed to work with the unique features and climate of the site.

The building was designed to use 10 percent of the potable water and 30 percent of the energy of a typical office building. Passive-solar principles and natural ventilation allow for the significant reduction of annual lighting and power needs. Natural resources are harvested daily including solar power through the building's photovoltaic panels, rainwater that is stored in reclaimed pickle barrels, and heat through a geothermal loop system. Water was conserved through the elimination of site irrigation with use of

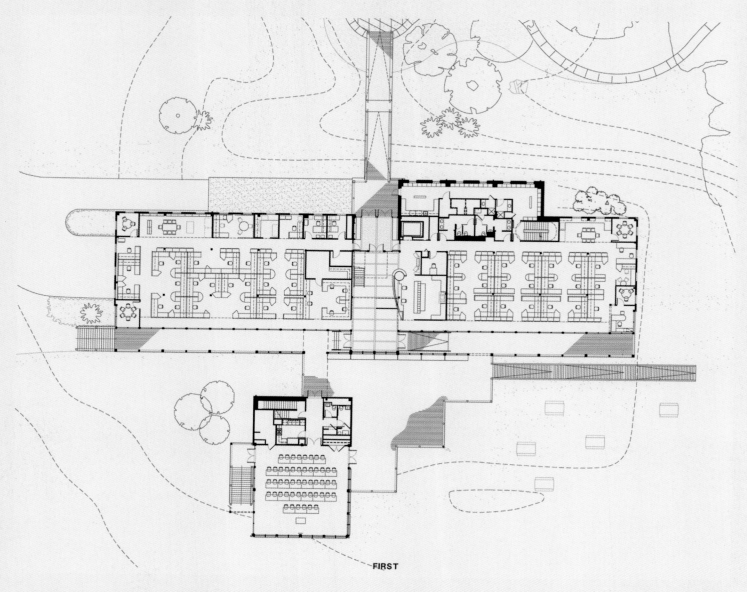

FIRST

native plant species, use of waterless composting toilets, and the implementation of a rainwater collection system that allows the reuse of this collected water in the fire suppression systems. The client supplemented the building systems with an innovative transportation management strategy that encourages more commuting by foot, bike, and boat. This reduced the size of the site needed to support the building by reducing the number of parking spaces needed.

Inside, the staff enjoys an inspirational, open-plan workplace full of daylight and exceptional air quality. The building materials chosen were either local, renewable or salvaged promoting a healthier work environment for the employees. Outside, the strategies for the building extend the surrounding site and bay ecosystem through the planting of native trees, wetlands, and by building an oyster reef. A holistic green approach to building allow for both the building occupants and surrounding habitat to thrive.

PREVIOUS PAGE: Exterior view of the building. The building integrates with sensitive bay ecosystem.

TOP: Floor plan.

RIGHT: Reclaimed pickle barrels are used as cisterns for rainwater collection.

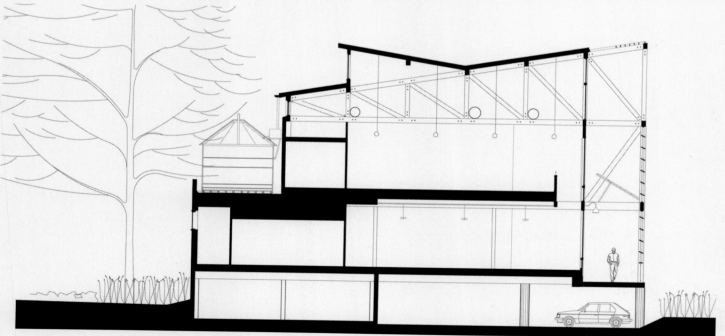

TOP LEFT: South facade showing the integration of solar panels.

BOTTOM LEFT: Building section.

TOP RIGHT: North elevation clad in galvanized siding made from cans, cars and other recycled material.

BOTTOM RIGHT: South elevation.

TOP LEFT: Life-cycle assessment informed the selection of all construction material for the building and the furniture used in the offices.

BOTTOM LEFT: Stair atrium and reception area.

RIGHT: The staff enjoys an inspirational, open-plan workplace full of daylight and natural ventilation.

Genzyme Center

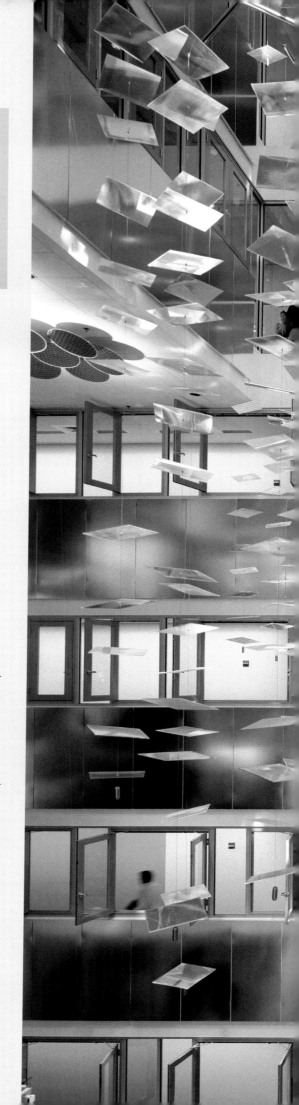

ARCHITECT: Behnisch Architekten

AREA: 336,555 Square Feet

LOCATION: Cambridge, Massachusetts

PHOTOGRAPHER: Anton Grassl

The headquarters for the world's third-largest bio-tech firm embodies a spirit of sustainable innovation in form and function. The design for this vibrant office environment calls to mind a small town, with squares, gardens and varied paths. The twelve office floors feature an open floor plan, allowing for varied office configurations that extend from the fully glazed perimeter of the building to the interior edge of a large central atrium. A series of 18 garden terraces border this inner courtyard and offer vegetated, daylight filled communal spaces to serve as alternative work areas. The open terraces set up visual connections and a sense of orientation for the employees and visitors.

Cascading through the center of the atrium is a hanging light refractor mobile, composed of mirrors and reflective surfaces that strategically bounce light deep into the building. To ensure an even distribution of light, a series of heliostats mounted on the roof, track the sun's movement and reflect light down to light refractor mirrors suspended throughout the space. These features were all a part of an innovative daylighting strategy to enable approximately 75 percent of the employees to work using only natural light.

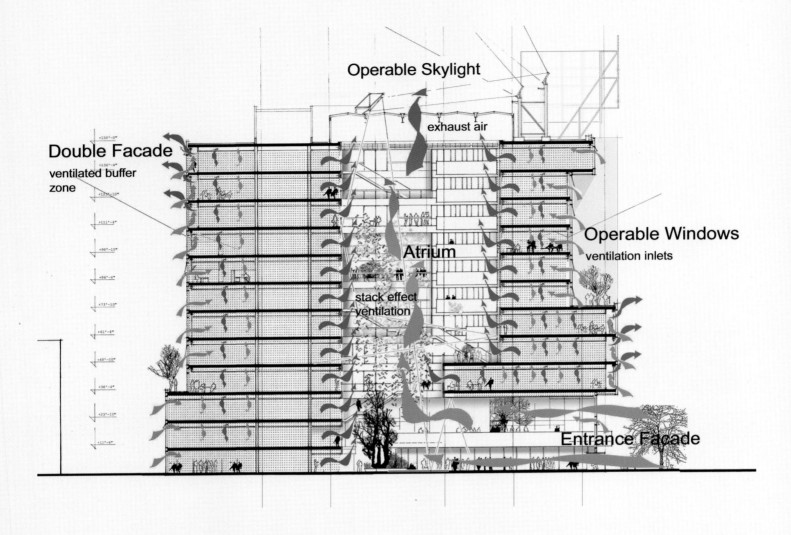

Double Facade
ventilated buffer zone

Operable Skylight

exhaust air

Atrium

stack effect ventilation

Operable Windows
ventilation inlets

Entrance Facade

The atrium design was also used as a part of an overall energy concept to lower operational and maintenance costs by naturally ventilating the building. The stack effect created by atrium volume helps to ventilate the building naturally by exhausting warm air through the roof via an operable skylight. This significantly reduced energy costs while providing a comfortable atmosphere for building occupants. Steam from a local power plant powers the central heating and mechanical cooling system further reducing the energy demand on the building. The exterior envelope is comprised of a high-performance curtain-wall glazing system and a double-walled facade. Sophisticated shading devices and solar collectors cover a third of the exterior envelope and provide optimum protection from solar heat gain in summer while capturing solar heat gains in the winter. The multi-faceted highly environmentally responsible building boasts a Platinum rating from the United States Green Building Council LEED certification program.

PREVIOUS PAGE: The atrium visually links together the building's various zones. Stairs between levels create physical connections.

TOP: Building section through the open atrium demonstrates how the building naturally ventilates hot air directly through the roof via an operable skylight.

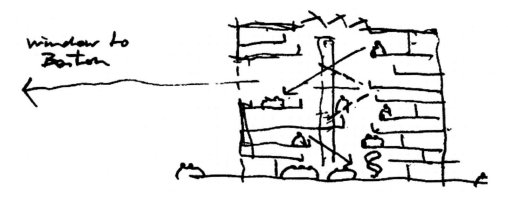

window to Boston

communication informal meeting

TOP: The high-performance curtain wall has operable windows that allow for additional ventilation in summer. The massing is punctuated with a corner tower and vertical solar panels.

LEFT: Conceptual sketch of the terraces and voids which provide occupants different views within and through the building.

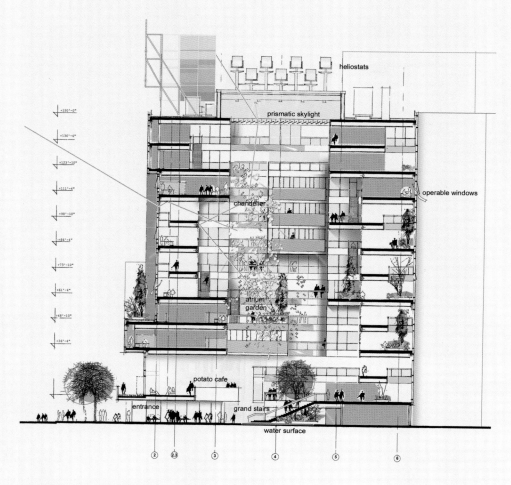

LEFT: This section shows how the design takes great advantage of natural daylight, with many offices having direct access to natural light. Roof-mounted solar panels, and an innovative cooling system, allows the building to use an estimated 25% less energy than a comparable building.

RIGHT: A light refractor doubles as a hanging sculpture that is composed reflective surfaces that bounce light throughout the interior.

BOTTOM LEFT: Interior gardens on each floor become flexible spaces for a variety of functions: from casual conversations to alternative meeting spaces.

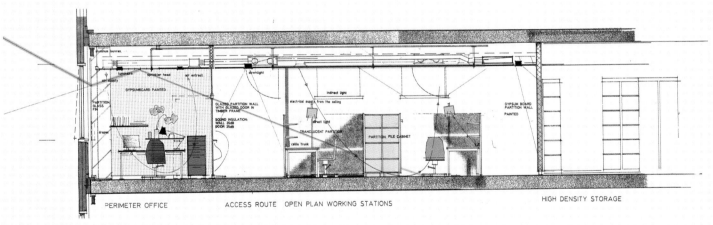

PERIMETER OFFICE   ACCESS ROUTE   OPEN PLAN WORKING STATIONS   HIGH DENSITY STORAGE

TOP LEFT: The interior cubicles are partly transparent, permitting light to filter into the core of the building.

BOTTOM LEFT: The transparent partitions are one of many features that allow approximately 75% of the employees to work using only natural light.

TOP RIGHT: All wood used in the construction and furniture is Forest Stewardship Council (FSC) certified, and 90 percent of all construction waste has been recycled. More than 75% of the building materials use recycled content, and more than half of the materials are from local (within 500 miles) sources.

BOTTOM RIGHT: Section illustrates how reflective window shades bounce light into the office space.

LEFT: View off upper floor of atrium.

RIGHT: Section illustrating how the light refractor bounces light throughout the interior.

BOTTOM RIGHT: Detail section at roof atrium and through levels ten to twelve.

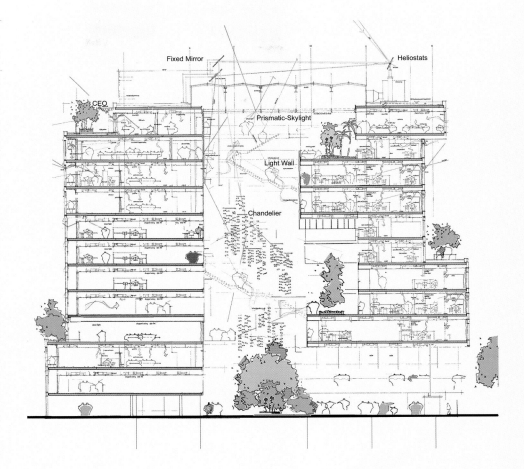

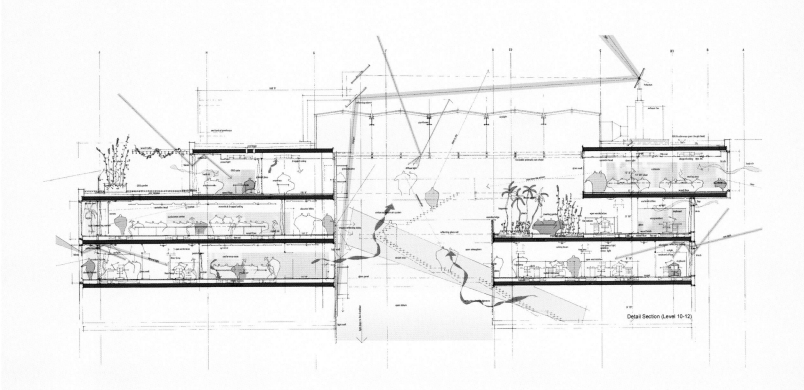

Herman Miller International UK Headquarters

ARCHITECT: Gensler

AREA: 20,000 Square Feet

LOCATION: Chippenham, United Kingdom

PHOTOGRAPHERS: Gensler/Hufton + Crow

As a leader in environmentally responsibile product design, Herman Miller sought to provide the greenest possible workplace for their international headquarters. The design delivers a sustainable facility in line with the company's long-standing belief that sustainable design is good business. The building and its surrounding landscape incorporate the latest sustainability strategies. It has been awarded an Excellent BREEAM rating and the U.S.G.B.C. LEED Gold certification. This innovative workplace accommodates 100 staff members within a combined office and showroom space.

A number of thermal modeling strategies were utilized to maximize natural energy sources. The building is oriented with the main spaces facing south. The north to south ventilation allows the building to breathe naturally and to cool passively. By naturally ventilating the building, the need for cooling towers and a humidification system was eliminated. Fresh air circulates throughout the building making the workplace a healthier environment to work in. The southern exposure lends itself to solar gains in winter and solar shading in summer. When natural sunlight is low, local switching and proximity detectors efficiently and economically light the

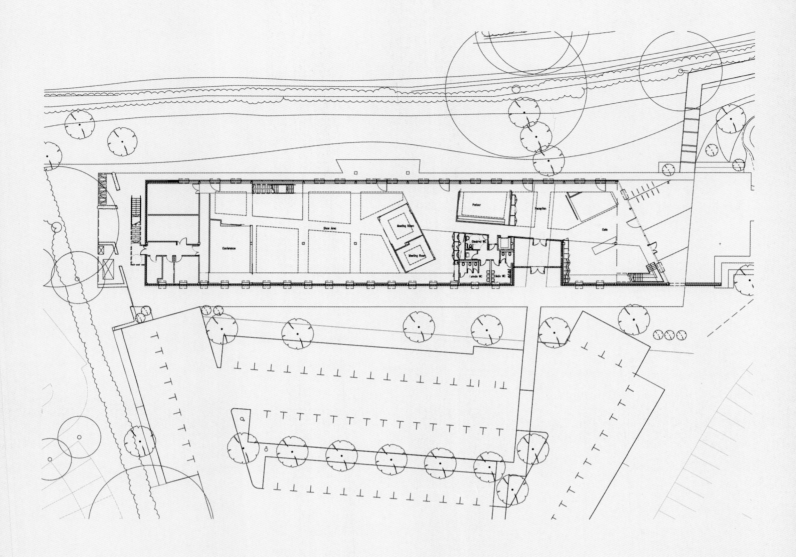

space with low energy fixtures. Various shading strategies were implemented to limit heat absorption into the building. A deep overhanging roof provides shade from direct sunlight for the building and exterior terrace. Concrete surfaces serve as thermal mass that help cool the building at night. Sensors monitor the temperature of these slabs to maintain a constant temperature within the building by remotely opening and closing windows.

Through implementation of time tested green strategies and an innovative approach to the contemporary workplace, the design for Herman Miller shows how investing in green technologies not only benefits the overall health of the employees but also the company's bottom line.

PREVIOUS PAGE: In the evening, when natural sunlight is low, local switching and proximity detectors efficiently and economically light the space with low energy fixtures.

TOP: Floor plan. The depth of the building is designed to maximize the floor plate while enabling efficient north to south cross ventilation.

RIGHT: Outdoor café seating serve as alternate work spaces and give occupants direct access to the outdoors.

TOP LEFT: The natural materials used—timber beams, junctions, ducts and floor slabs—are exposed to eliminate the need for plasterboard and applied finishes that are considered pollutants.

BOTTOM LEFT: Natural light in the interior is maximized by using full-height glazing. Glare from the sun is avoided by the individual internal blinds and deep overhangs.

RIGHT: Thick stone-clad walls to the south protect the building from the heat of the sun and keep the building cool.

TOP: Flexible work settings range from conventional desks to the comfortable lounge seating.

BOTTOM LEFT: The workplace is also a showroom and is used as a tool in the selling process.

BOTTOM FAR RIGHT: Full height glazing along the north facade provides consistent indirect daylighting into the office.

BOTTOM RIGHT: Breakout spaces are furnished with all Herman Miller products.

Kitsap County Administration Building

ARCHITECT: Miller Hull Partnership

AREA: 70,000 Square Feet

LOCATION: Port Orchard, Washington

PHOTOGRAPHER: Nic Lehoux & Miller Hull

A challenging site informs the sustainable design approach of the new anchor building for the Kitsap County government campus. The design response to a 55' grade change was to terrace the building into the hillside. This allowed for multiple narrow north-facing floor plates while providing water views for nearly every occupant. The building houses five departments, organized around a three-story lobby that visually and functionally connects the building to the main civic plaza and Commissioners meeting room, the heart of the civic campus. This dramatic lobby, lit from a linear skylight above, is flanked by cast-in-place concrete walls that anchor the balconies and the ceremonial main stair.

A range of sustainable strategies from rainwater collection to recycled content materials were used to reduce the overall embodied and operational energy of the building. A fly ash concrete superstructure retains the steep slope and provides a solid deck for nearly an acre of green roof. Five concrete rainwater cisterns, located beneath exterior stair landings, collect water runoff from the roofs, that is used for site irrigation in the dry season. A narrow footprint combined with skylights at the rear of office spaces allow daylight to penetrate into the earth-sheltered portions of

the building. Remote light sensors read outside light levels and dim the lights accordingly to reduce overall artificial lighting needs.

The concrete structure provides tremendous thermal mass that minimizes temperature fluctuations throughout the daily cycle. An under-floor air distribution system utilizes the cooler temperature of the previous night, delaying the cooling cycle well into the workday. It has exceeded the occupant's performance expectations; in the first winter of operation only one of the two boilers was activated.

PREVIOUS PAGE: A two-story steel canopy on the south facade provides shade and a dramatic civic entrance.

TOP: Main entrance at night.

UPPER RIGHT: Floor plan. The narrow 30' plan allows daylight to penetrate into the earth-sheltered portions of the building.

MIDDLE RIGHT: Site section showing the steep 55' site elevation change.

LOWER RIGHT: West Elevation at stair.

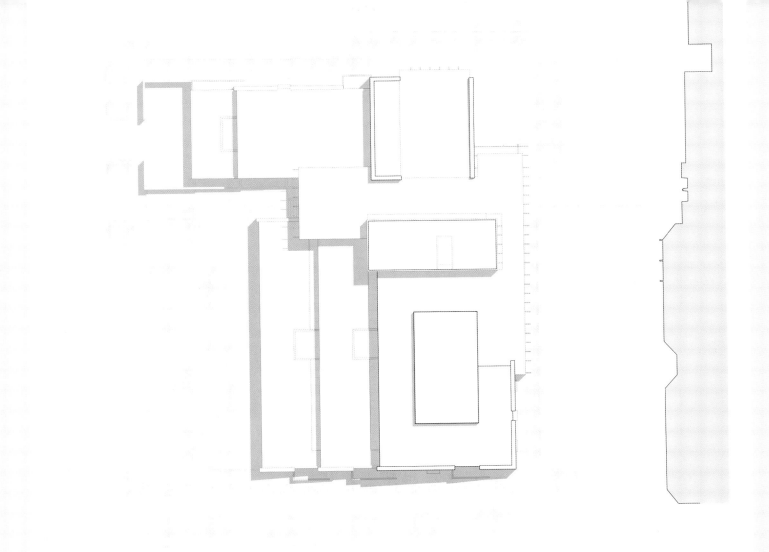

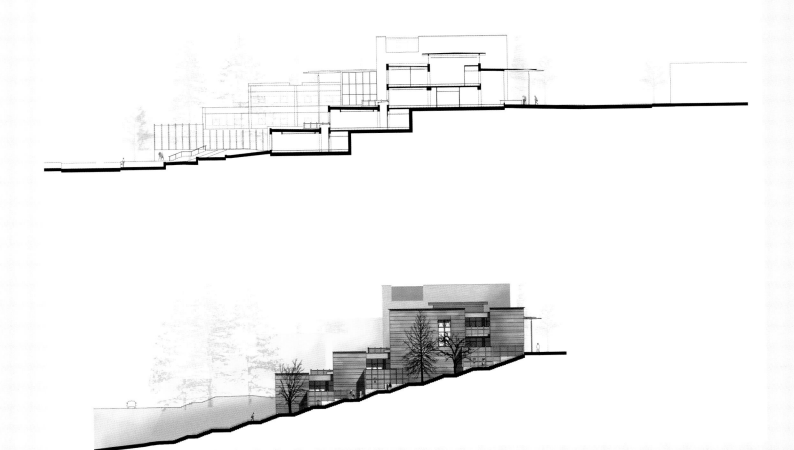

LEFT: The main lobby of the building is a three-story space that is lit from a linear skylight above.

TOP RIGHT: Full height windows allow for natural daylight to filter into work areas while deep overhangs eliminate glare from direct sunlight.

BOTTOM FAR RIGHT: Nearly an acre of green roofs and generously landscaped areas reduce site storm water retention requirements.

BOTTOM RIGHT: The five departments that occupy the building are connected by a light filled atrium and stair.

TOP LEFT: The use of low and zero VOC materials helps protect indoor air quality.

BOTTOM LEFT: Light bounces off of the light colored ceiling surfaces.

RIGHT: Linear skylights over circulation spaces allow for minimal use of artificial lighting which effectively conserves energy throughout the day.

Save The Bay Educational Center

ARCHITECT: Croxton Collaborative Architects

AREA: 15,000 Square Feet

LOCATION: Providence, Rhode Island

PHOTOGRAPHER: Ruggero Vanni

The Bay Educational Center embodies Save The Bay's mission to act as stewards of the Narragansett Bay and its watershed by designing a site sensitive response that protects the bay ecology. Their innovative program has provided 65,000 children with their first experience out on the water. Built on an old junkyard site, the project became a recipient of the EPA's Phoenix Award for the best brownfield reclamation in Region One. A one-story linear design was selected to respond to the horizontality of the site and orientation toward the bay. Mirroring the programmatic split between administrative/advocacy and education programs, the building is composed of two wings connected by a central lobby. Public spaces are located to the south to maximize views and access to daylight while support spaces are organized to the north against the berm.

The program is organized around the path of the sun by locating the administrative program to the east (morning activities) and educational programs to the west (afternoon activities). Subsequently, occupied spaces are oriented toward the south to maximize daylight and views while storage and support spaces are on the north side, with the earthen berm, to support a thermally stable environment.

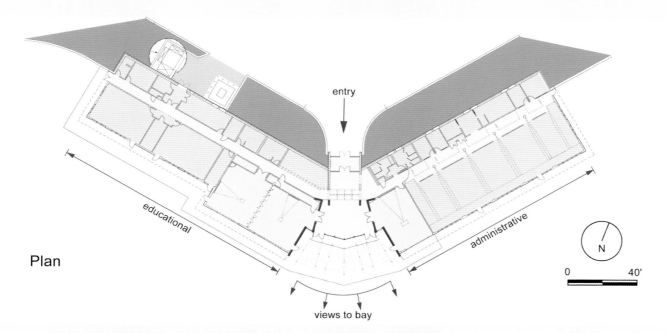

entry

educational

administrative

N

0   40'

Plan

views to bay

The building section facilitates natural cross-ventilation by locating operable windows and doors at grade and the operable clerestory windows above. Integrated seamlessly with its Narragansett Bay site, this project accentuates a visual and physical connection to the outdoor environment. This connection was emphasized by utilizing 14 different glazed exits and large windows in all major spaces facing south. Integrated with this fenestration strategy, two rows of clerestory windows in the administrative wing bring light deep into the building.

Internally, the building implements many water-conserving fixtures. Waterless urinals and dual-flush toilets conserve water and also introduce these technologies to the public. The building has a 20kW photovoltaic array on the south roof that produces enough power to the entire lighting system for the whole year. With an eye toward the future, the gas-fired mechanical system can shift to bio-fuel or other fuels when markets or client intentions shift.

PREVIOUS PAGE: The horizontality of the coastal edge and water is an inherent character of the site. On the south facade, high-performance glazing allows for passive solar heating in the winter while deep south-facing eaves reduce overheating in the summer.

TOP: The plan of the 15,000 sf building is composed of two wings connected by a central lobby which mirrors the programmatic split between administrative/advocacy and education programs. Public spaces are located to the south to maximize views and access to daylight while support spaces are organized to the north against the berm.

TOP RIGHT: A 7,000 sf north-facing green roof absorbs stormwater and insulates the envelope. Any additional runoff is absorbed in swales/raingardens below.

MIDDLE RIGHT: The entrance to the center allows for a transparent view towards the ocean.

LOWER RIGHT: Cross section. The sloping green roof and connected swales/raingardens allow for the site to manage all of the stormwater (5-year storm) onsite to protect the bay ecology while providing an attractive aesthetic feature to the building.

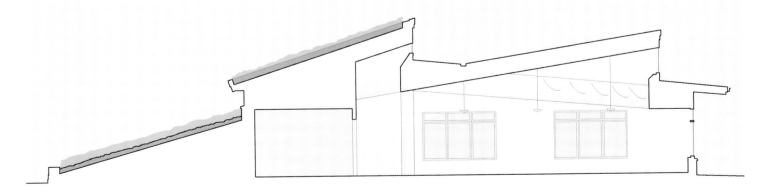

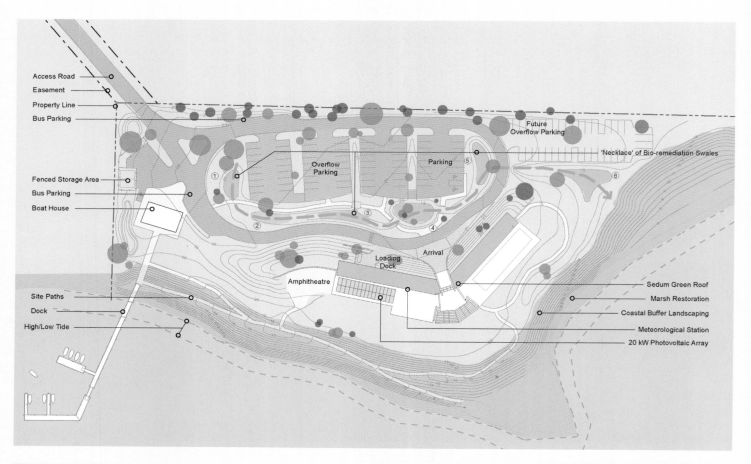

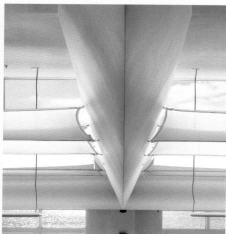

TOP: Sustainable site strategy plan.

BOTTOM FAR LEFT: Zero-VOC paints and varnishes, low-VOC carpet and linoleum are the primary interior materials in the project. In addition, the office systems furniture is Greenseal certified.

BOTTOM LEFT: Daylight is diffused through suspended sail canopy.

TOP RIGHT: Salt marsh restoration areas.

MIDDLE RIGHT: 100% of the granite at the amphitheater was harvested from the site.

LOWER RIGHT: Trellis diffuses direct sunlight and provides a sheltered space for eating and socializing, while the outdoor amphitheater offers a vantage point to admire the view.

901 Cherry

OFFICES FOR GAP INC.

ARCHITECT: William McDonough + Partners

AREA: 195,000 Square Feet

LOCATION: San Bruno, California

PHOTOGRAPHER: Mark Luthringer

Originally designed for Gap Inc., 901 Cherry in San Bruno, California is a superb example of how a large office building can achieve a sustainable vision. The footprint of the impressive 195,000 square foot building would have displaced an area of land home to many birds and creatures. In response to this reality, a green roof system retains native grasses and wildflowers that would have otherwise been removed. The gently curving green roofs seek to make birds flying overhead think that nothing on the site had changed.

To ensure healthy indoor air quality for the employees, an energy efficient under-floor air distribution system (UFAD) was used. An UFAD system delivers cool air low in the occupied areas of the space and exhausts the air high. Since warm air rises naturally, the building does not need to rely on the mechanical system to push the air throughout the space. In addition, conventional mechanical systems supply air from above and cover up the ductwork with suspended ceilings. Since the UFAD ductwork is below the floor, it enables flexible cable management and for the suspended ceiling to be eliminated. The ceilings become uncluttered with only lights and sprinklers visible and the taller ceiling heights allow for better daylight distribution. As a result, the building further reduces its material and energy consumption.

The building was recognized by Pacific Gas and Electric as the second-most energy-efficient building in the state and exceeds California's strict energy requirements by 30 percent. The light-filled warm office space cultivates a sense of community through its openness of the design, circulation paths, and common spaces and because of this, the building and its employees thrive.

PREVIOUS PAGE: Exterior elevation at night. Night-time ventilation was a key component in providing a low-energy system.

TOP: Three undulating green roofs are the defining features of the building.

TOP RIGHT: Site plan showing the extents of green roof.

BOTTOM RIGHT: Aerial view of the Green Roofs. The mass of the soil acts as an acoustic barrier to noise from the nearby airport.

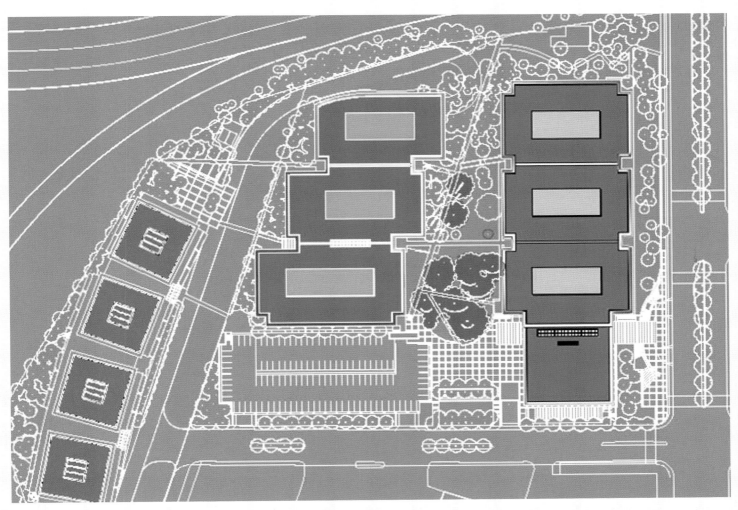

LEFT: The office spaces in the building are organized around a double height 30' x 90' atrium. The roof monitor provides daylighting and aids in the natural ventilation of the building

TOP RIGHT: The workplace looking out onto expansive green roof fosters a visual connection to the outdoor environment.

BOTTOM RIGHT: Section diagram of roof monitor.

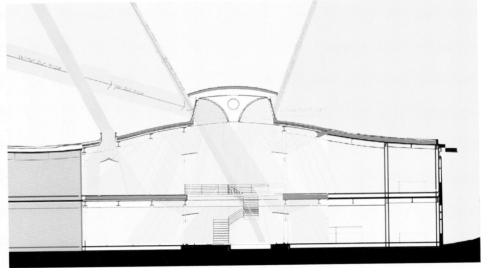

LEFT: The patio invites occupants to enjoy extensive outdoor communal spaces.

TOP RIGHT: Interior finishes included concrete café counters with recycled content, low VOC paints, and table tops and benches made from eucalyptus trees removed from the site before construction.

BOTTOM RIGHT: Natural daylight from an overhead skylight floods into informal waiting areas.

SC3

■ ■ ■

ARCHITECT: Smith Carter Architects and Engineers
AREA: 47,635 Square Feet
LOCATION: Winnipeg, Manitoba, Canada
PHOTOGRAPHER: Gerry Kopelow

A multi-disciplinary design firm showcases their commitment to sustainability by designing an environmentally-sensitive intellectually-stimulating workplace. The long rectilinear building is sited among Manitoba Prairie grassland on the edge of a preserved spruce forest. The open site allowed for the use of an open loop geothermal cooling and heating system driven by heat pumps that significantly reduce energy consumption for the entire building. The geothermal system radiantly heats the building and provides a level of thermal comfort not typical for an office environment. The site also accommodated a detention pond that reduces the load on city storm water system. Together with the use of other water efficiency features such as dual flush toilets, waterless urinals and low flow faucet's, showerheads and dishwasher's, the building uses 290,000 liters less water per year than a conventional office building.

Other sustainable strategies were employed such as enforcing an Indoor Air Quality Management Plan which safeguarded the health of workers during construction. This strategy extended to the health of their employees by only specifying earth-friendly building materials. The simple rectilinear box design, with expansive glass windows, frame the spruce

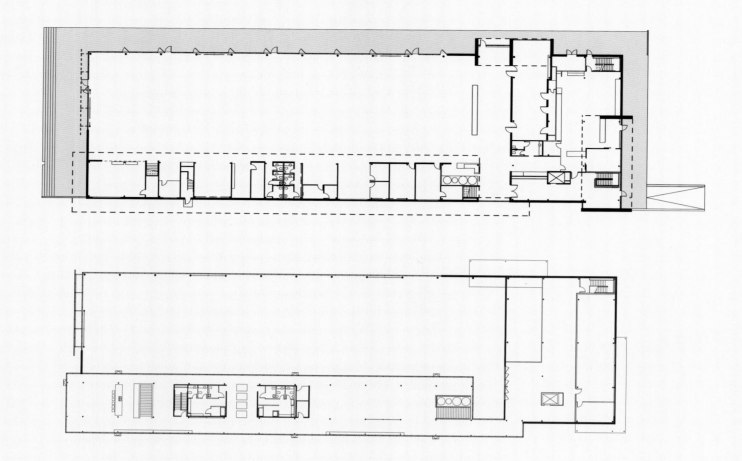

forest and provides 95 percent of the workers with direct views to the outdoors. Natural daylight pours into the space and contributes to a sense of well-being and workplace effectiveness. The design studio is the core, with a cantilevered skybox above that serves as collaborative work areas and community space. The open floor plan and under floor air distribution system allow for an open and flexible studio environment. The simple double height cross-section allows for natural ventilation to be used. Motorized windows connected to the mechanical system open to exhaust hot air when environmental conditions necessitate.   The result is a building that surpasses the energy requirements of the Canadian Model National Energy Code for Buildings by 55 percent while simultaneously provide a home where creativity can flourish.

PREVIOUS PAGE: South deck screen. Exterior lighting has been designed to virtually eliminate light spill from the site. This ensures an energy efficient exterior lighting approach that does not contribute to light pollution of the night sky.

ABOVE: Main level floor plan.

TOP: Second floor plan.

TOP RIGHT: A horizontal box cantilevers over the prairie grassland acting as a suspended billboard to the highway traffic beyond. The landscape design promoted biodiversity by creating a habitat and food supply for bats, birds and other species.

BOTTOM RIGHT: The mechanical air intake is on the tree side of the building so fresh air is filtered by the spruce forest before entering the building.

TOP LEFT: The gallery and skybox.

MIDDLE LEFT: Operable window at skybox helps to naturally ventilate building.

BOTTOM LEFT: Natural ventilation cross-section diagram. Motorized windows and clerestories that tie into the building's automation system allow natural ventilation when outdoor ambient conditions permit.

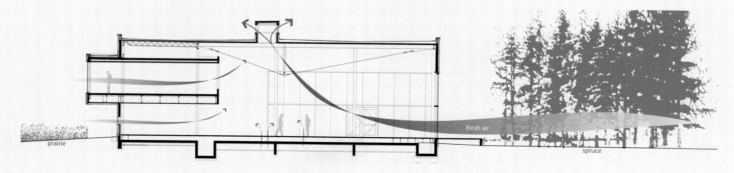

prairie

fresh air

spruce

TOP RIGHT: Steel kingpin trusses allow for a flexible office layout.

BOTTOM RIGHT: Thermal diagram.

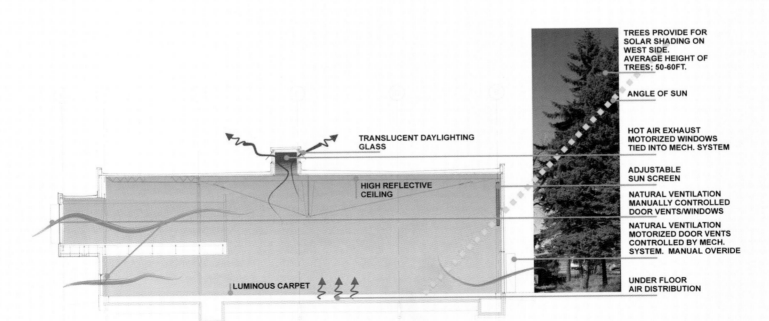

TRANSLUCENT DAYLIGHTING GLASS

HIGH REFLECTIVE CEILING

LUMINOUS CARPET

TREES PROVIDE FOR SOLAR SHADING ON WEST SIDE. AVERAGE HEIGHT OF TREES; 50-60FT.

ANGLE OF SUN

HOT AIR EXHAUST MOTORIZED WINDOWS TIED INTO MECH. SYSTEM

ADJUSTABLE SUN SCREEN

NATURAL VENTILATION MANUALLY CONTROLLED DOOR VENTS/WINDOWS

NATURAL VENTILATION MOTORIZED DOOR VENTS CONTROLLED BY MECH. SYSTEM. MANUAL OVERIDE

UNDER FLOOR AIR DISTRIBUTION

TOP LEFT: The client entry and deck. The decks and walking paths surrounding the building mediate technology and nature—a transition between work and leisure, building and landscape.

BOTTOM LEFT: Corrugated steel panels clad the exterior west facade.

TOP RIGHT: The studio frames the spruce forest, filling the space with natural light and eliminating the need for artificial lighting overhead.

BOTTOM RIGHT: All existing trees preserve and frame the client entrance to the building.

Kresge Foundation Headquarters

ARCHITECT: Valerio Dewalt Train Associates

AREA: 19,000 Square Feet

LOCATION: Troy, Michigan

PHOTOGRAPHERS: Barbara Karant & Justin Maconochie

A non-profit organization that awards grants across the country, uses their new headquarters building to bring visibility to sustainable design and site conservation awareness. Committed to remain at their present site, the Kresge Foundation utilized a 19th century farmhouse, barn and other agricultural structures to expand their building preserve. The original stone farmhouse welcomes visitors as a reception and consultation space, and staff meetings are held in the barn. A new modern addition, clad in metal panels and glass, is nestled among the existing structures and a constructed wetland. Grassy embankments obscure neighboring buildings and highways while preserving views to the ponds and landscape.

All of the water needed for landscaping is obtained through direct rainfall or rainwater collected by a cistern. Any excess water is diverted into a system of bioswales (shallow, vegetation-filled channels flowing around the property) and constructed wetlands that encourage further percolation into the site. In the process, rainwater is naturally filtered. The long native prairie grasses are also highly absorbent, allowing for reductions in the size of retention ponds.

The new structure is partially covered by four green roofs, each populated with drought-resistant native plants. A geothermal heating and cooling system was chosen with forty geothermal wells that extend 400 feet

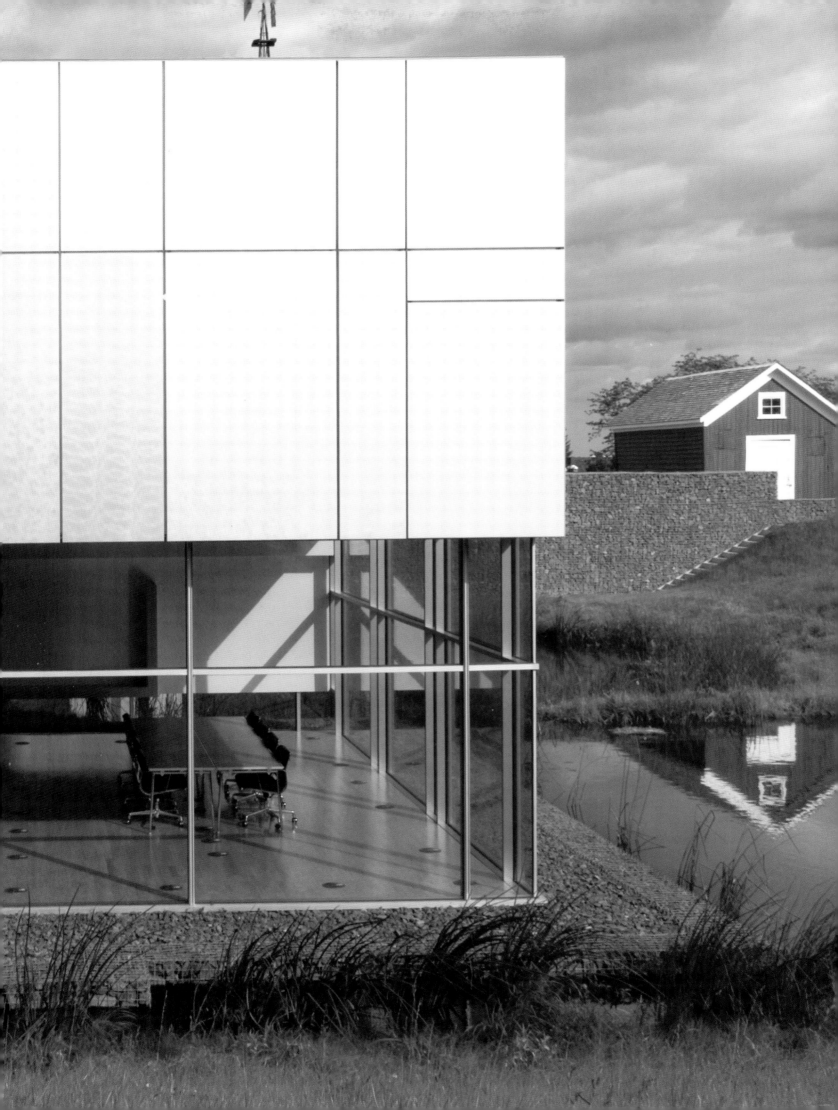

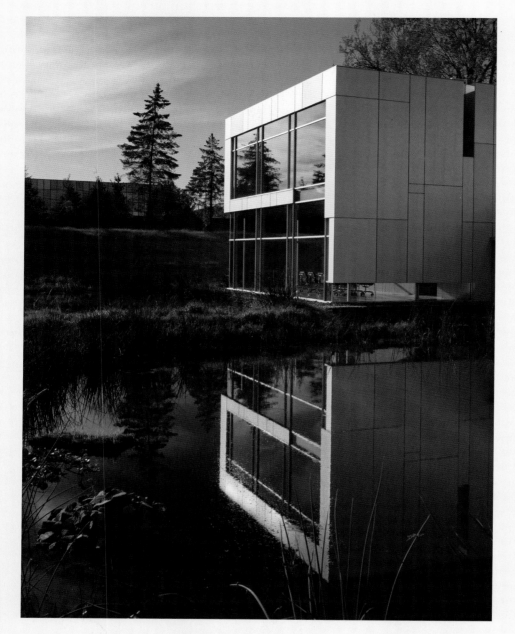

into the earth and are located below the parking area. By embedding large portions of the office building in the earth, the site relies on many retaining walls for structure. These walls were formed with gabions as an alternative to traditional concrete retaining walls. These gabion walls are composed of recycled concrete and crushed granite found on site and are enclosed in a steel mesh.

Though a building does not have to be LEED certified to be green, Kresge decided to obtain certification because this documentation would lend credibility to their building as a model for non-profits considering to build sustainably. The Kresge staff has adopted the behaviors required to achieve the building's intended economic, health and environmental benefits. They continue to implement sustainable practices on a daily basis—from using recycled and recyclable office supplies to carpooling.

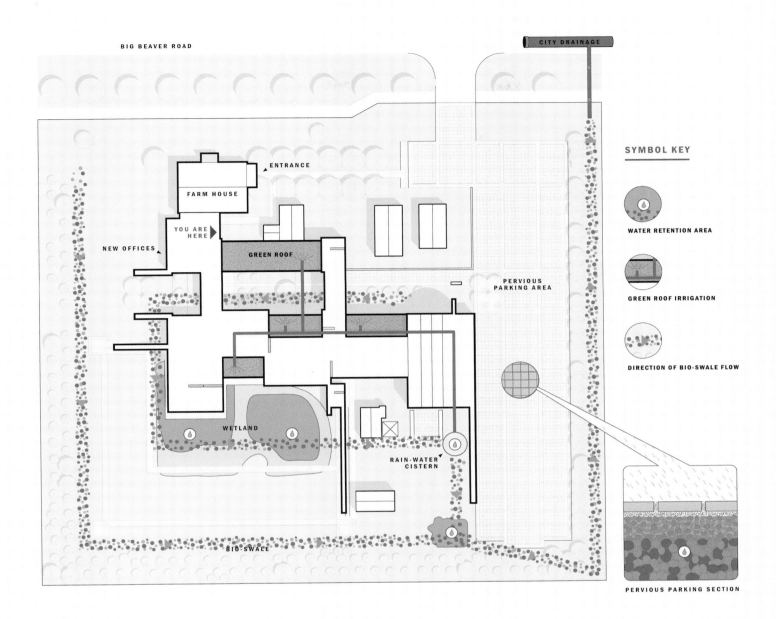

BIG BEAVER ROAD

CITY DRAINAGE

ENTRANCE

FARM HOUSE

YOU ARE HERE ▶

NEW OFFICES

GREEN ROOF

PERVIOUS PARKING AREA

WETLAND

RAIN-WATER CISTERN

BIO-SWALE

SYMBOL KEY

WATER RETENTION AREA

GREEN ROOF IRRIGATION

DIRECTION OF BIO-SWALE FLOW

PERVIOUS PARKING SECTION

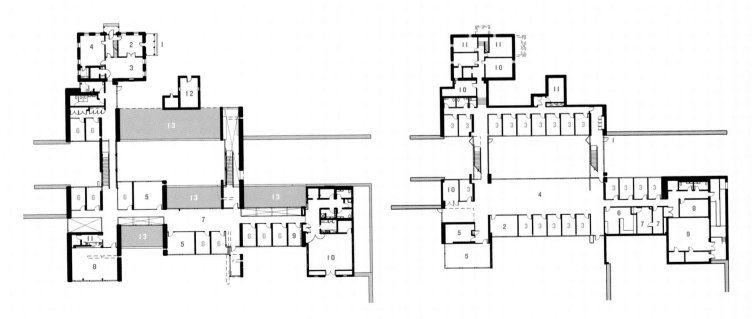

LEFT: Walls are coated with "milk paint" that is made from milk protein, herbs and minerals and contains no volatile organic compounds (VOCs).

TOP RIGHT: Drought-resistant and native plants were chosen for landscaping and green roofs. For the most part, they survive naturally without the need for irrigation systems.

BOTTOM RIGHT: Conference rooms overlooking the constructed wetlands.

TOP LEFT: All of the water needed for landscaping is obtained through direct rainfall or rainwater collected by a cistern located next to the existing barn.

LOWER LEFT: New and old are woven into a symbiotic campus.

RIGHT: Innovative retaining walls filled with demolition waste. This strategy saved about half the cost of conventional concrete retaining walls.

LEFT: An open office allows for maximum daylight and air circulation.

TOP RIGHT: Wood flooring and desks are made of rapidly renewable wheat board finished with a veneer of FSC-certified sustainably harvested wood.

BOTTOM RIGHT: Enclosed offices are transparent to allow for daylight to penetrate deep into the building.

National Resource Defense Council Office

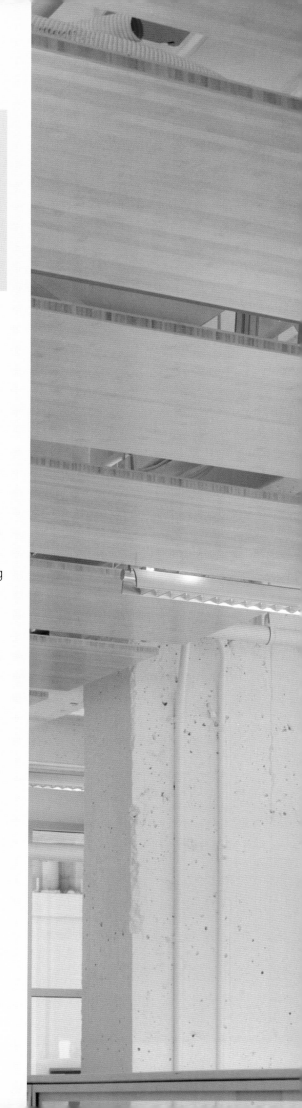

ARCHITECT: Leddy Maytum Stacy Architects

AREA: 19,700 Square Feet

LOCATION: San Francisco, California

PHOTOGRAPHER: Cesar Rubio

The design for the NRDC office demonstrates that energy-efficient, environmentally responsible workplaces are simply good business. While the sustainable building movement has focused mainly on new, freestanding construction, until recently a huge portion of our nation's annual construction activity has been largely ignored: office tenant improvements within existing structures. For this reason, the Natural Resources Defense Council decided to make their new San Francisco offices a case study of the affordable, environmentally-responsible workplace built within an existing office building. The host building, built in 1927 (before air conditioning and fluorescent lighting were invented), was selected for its many built-in features, including operable windows, abundant natural light, narrow floor plates, and proximity to major transit lines. Daylighting and view strategies, natural and mechanical ventilation systems, lighting systems and controls, sustainable materials and assemblies are all integral to the architectural character of the space. Bathed in natural light and filled with clean air throughout the day, the interior spaces provide a positive work environment for the employees.

The project demonstrates that sustainable office interiors can be affordable for organizations and businesses of all types. The design team

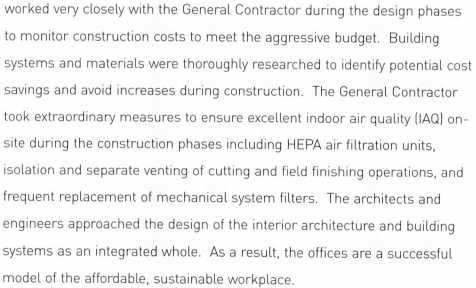

worked very closely with the General Contractor during the design phases to monitor construction costs to meet the aggressive budget. Building systems and materials were thoroughly researched to identify potential cost savings and avoid increases during construction. The General Contractor took extraordinary measures to ensure excellent indoor air quality (IAQ) on-site during the construction phases including HEPA air filtration units, isolation and separate venting of cutting and field finishing operations, and frequent replacement of mechanical system filters. The architects and engineers approached the design of the interior architecture and building systems as an integrated whole. As a result, the offices are a successful model of the affordable, sustainable workplace.

PREVIOUS PAGE: Renewable materials, including bamboo door veneers, casework and suspended ceiling panels, total 17% of the material cost of the project.

FAR LEFT: Due to strategic space planning ample daylight and city views area available from 90% of the interior spaces.

LEFT: Reception area and stair railing use resin panels made from recycled milk jugs.

RIGHT: 20th and 21st floor plans. The narrow floor plate, tall ceilings and windows were used to amplify daylight penetration.

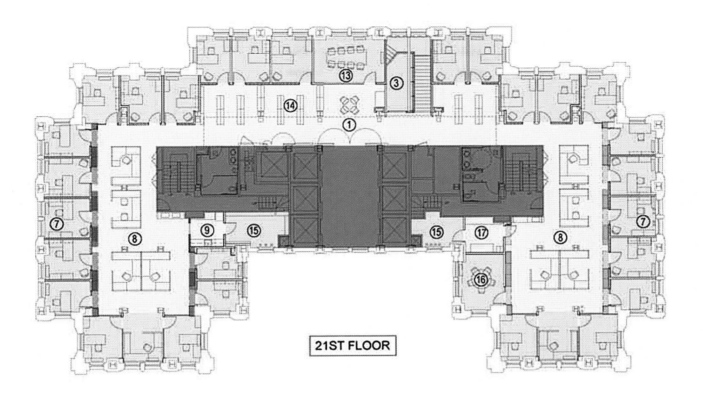

21ST FLOOR

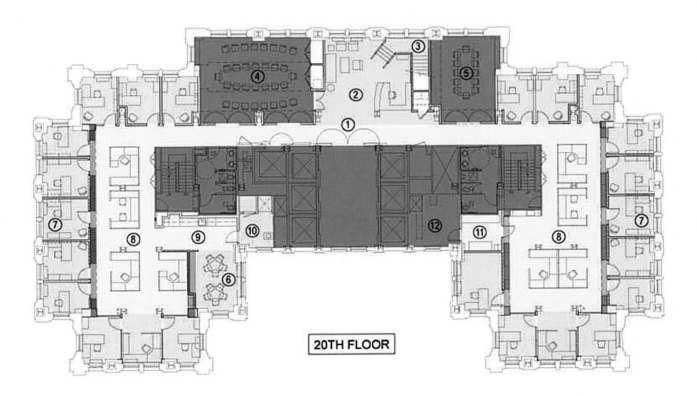

20TH FLOOR

BUILDING CORE

"THICK WALL"

NATURAL VENTILATION AREA

REVISED MECHANICAL VENTILATION AREA

ENERGY EFFICIENT AIR CONDITIONED AREA

1. MAIN ENTRANCE / CORRIDOR
2. RECEPTION
3. STAIR
4. LARGE CONFERENCE ROOM
5. MEDIUM CONFERENCE ROOM
6. SMALL CONFERENCE / BREAK ROOM
7. PERIMETER OFFICES
8. OPEN OFFICES
9. KITCHEN
10. SHOWER

11. COPY / SUPPLY ROOM
12. SERVER
13. VIDEO CONFERENCE ROOM
14. LAW LIBRARY
15. STORAGE
16. SMALL COFERENCE ROOM
17. COPY / MAIL

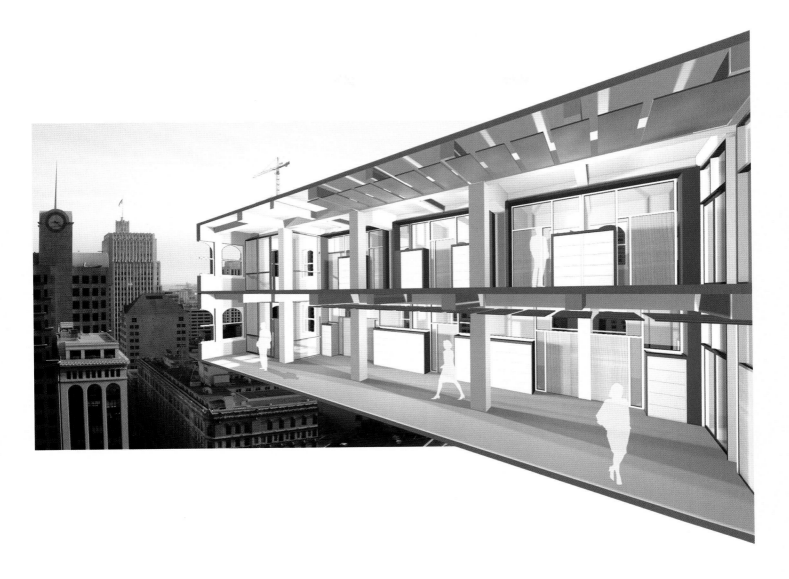

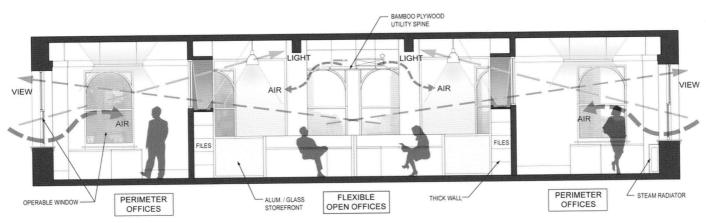

BAMBOO PLYWOOD
UTILITY SPINE

LIGHT — LIGHT

VIEW — AIR — AIR — VIEW

AIR — FILES — FILES — AIR

OPERABLE WINDOW — PERIMETER OFFICES — ALUM. / GLASS STOREFRONT — FLEXIBLE OPEN OFFICES — THICK WALL — PERIMETER OFFICES — STEAM RADIATOR

TOP LEFT: Clerestory glazing at partition walls between the perimeter offices permit infiltration of daylight into the space.

BOTTOM LEFT: The interior workspaces use PVC-free carpet, low-VOC paints and adhesives, and formaldehyde-free wood products. New and custom furniture use FSC-certified woods and environmentally friendly fabrics.

TOP RIGHT: Axonometric of of office showing partition walls with clerestory windows.

BOTTOM RIGHT: Cross section through the office space. Perimeter offices use existing windows for ventilation and radiators for heat. Interior workspaces utilize the existing mechanical systems.

White Rock Operations Building

■ ■ ■ ■

ARCHITECT: Busby Perkins + Will
AREA: 6,545 Square Feet
LOCATION: White Rock, British Columbia, Canada
PHOTOGRAPHERS: Colin Jewall & Enrico Dagostini

An abondoned sanitary treatment plant became the foundation for Canada's first new construction LEED Gold building. The winning entry in a competition, hosted by the City of White Rock, mandated that the new operations building be as green as possible. The first step in achieving the mandate was to reuse the abandoned facility's existing storage tanks as the building's foundation. The building developed into two separate pavilions: a two-story component on the north end, housing departmental elements which are only periodically used (field crew facilities, change rooms, meeting and lunch rooms), and a one-story building on the south end, housing the offices for the department.

A green roof absorbs rain and additional stormwater runoff is used for toilets and waterless urinals. Solar photovoltaic panels on the roof and solar tubes mounted to the side of the structure reduce energy consumption and the future tax burden on city residents. Reclaimed woods and low-VOC emitting materials were used throughout the interior office environment effectively eliminating the potential for toxic off-gassing

Collectively, these innovative sustainable strategies have significantly reduced site water use by approximately 90%, and energy consumption by 60% exceeding the standards set by the Canadian Model National Energy Code.

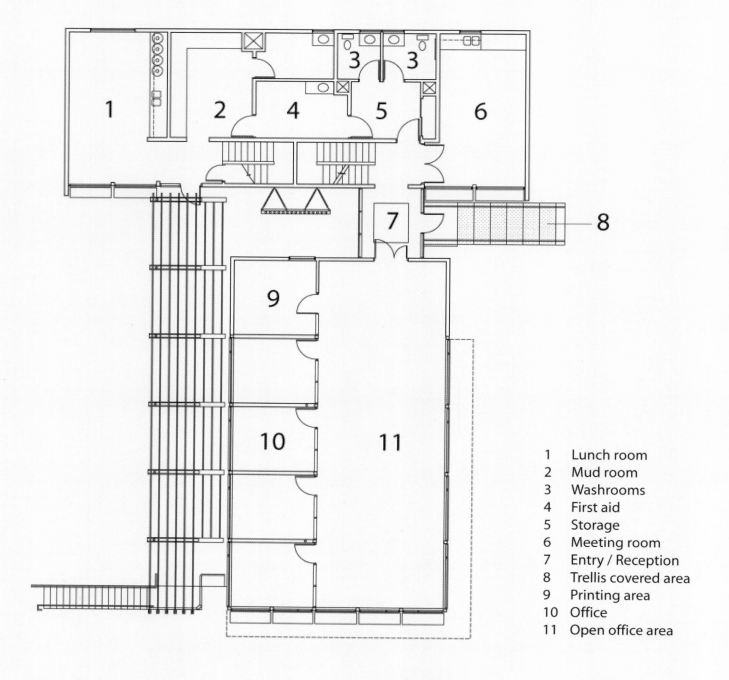

1 Lunch room
2 Mud room
3 Washrooms
4 First aid
5 Storage
6 Meeting room
7 Entry / Reception
8 Trellis covered area
9 Printing area
10 Office
11 Open office area

As a result, the City of White Rock Operations Building was certified
LEED Gold, making it only the second building in Canada to achieve this
standing and the first for new construction. Subsequently, it the building won
the Medal for Excellence and numerous other sustainable awards.

PREVIOUS PAGE: Exterior entry. The exterior envelope is clad in red cedar, cementitious wall panels & glass.

TOP LEFT: Floor plan.

TOP RIGHT: The entrance to the building is between the two separate pavilions: a two-story component on the north end, housing departmental elements that are only periodically used and a one-story building on the south end, housing the office component of the department.

BOTTOM RIGHT: The design incorporated the reuse of existing foundations of the abandoned sanitary treatment plant.

TOP LEFT: Sun shading trellises were used for shading and to diffuse light along window walls year-round.

BOTTOM LEFT: A planted roof is built over a recycled heavy timber roof structure

RIGHT: Wall section at sun shade.

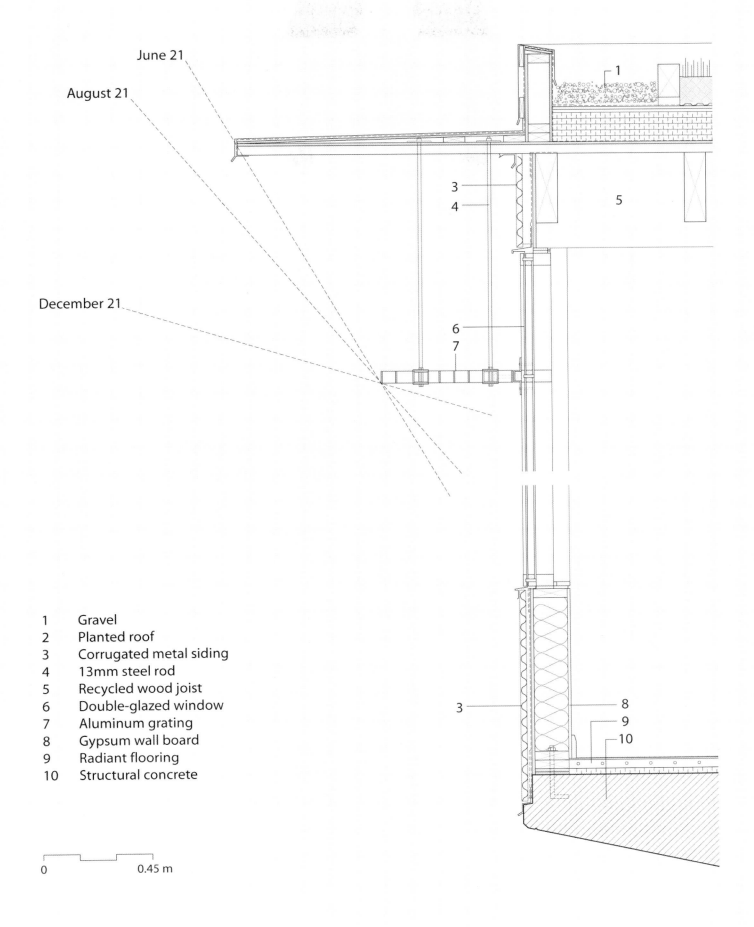

June 21

August 21

December 21

1   Gravel
2   Planted roof
3   Corrugated metal siding
4   13mm steel rod
5   Recycled wood joist
6   Double-glazed window
7   Aluminum grating
8   Gypsum wall board
9   Radiant flooring
10   Structural concrete

0   0.45 m

TOP LEFT: Exposed reclaimed beams add warmth to the interior and eliminate unnecessary drywall material that would have been used for a dropped ceiling.

BOTTOM LEFT: Photovoltaic arrays.

BOTTOM RIGHT: Low partition walls allow daylight to penetrate into the office space.

TOP RIGHT: Solar tubes for heating, reduced energy consumption.

Bonheiden Police Administrative Center

ARCHITECT: VBM Architecten

AREA: 46,600 Square Feet

LOCATION: Blikveld Bonheiden, Belgium

PHOTOGRAPHER: Toon Grobet

The design for the new Administrative Center for the City of Bonheiden Police demonstrates how sustainable design strategies can inform the overall expression of a building. A raised two-story volume perched on concrete columns and skinned in a series of galvanized steel mesh sun screens are the defining characteristics of the building. The screens serve a dual purpose of reducing glare and filtering daylight into the interior work spaces, but also provide privacy and visual protection to the police employees. Each semi-transparent steel mesh screen pivots manually towards the average solar position in order to combine shading with a view to the landscape. During the day, the employees have access to privately screened shaded exterior walkways that allows for them to see out, but others not to see in. In the evening, the outer skin becomes almost invisible, the interior is revealed to the public outside.

On the roof, photovoltaic panels provide auxiliary power and enough energy for hot water service for the entire building while rainwater runoff is stored in concrete cisterns for use in toilets and fire protection. A central atrium allows light to penetrate two levels of the central circulation areas while further functioning to reduce energy consumption by allowing for natural

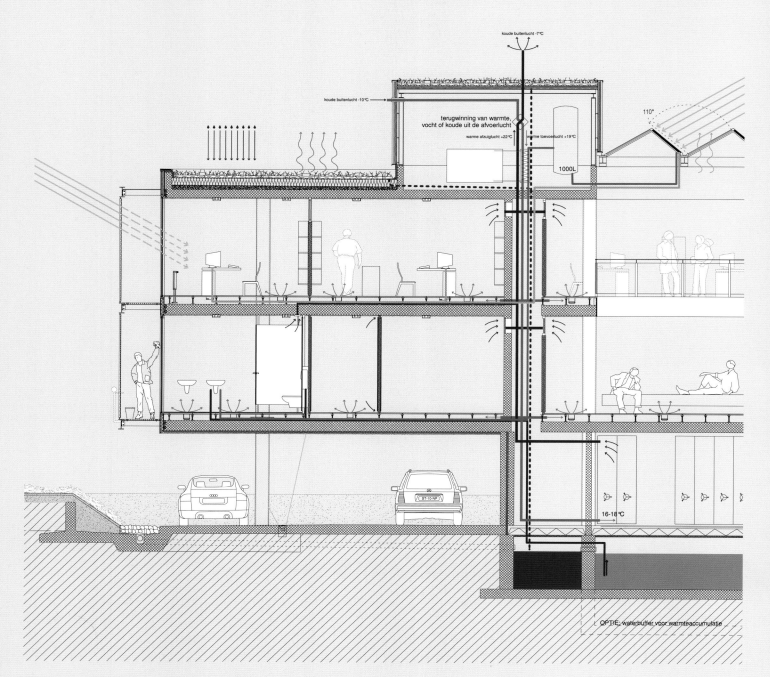

Labels on drawing:

koude buitenlucht -7°C

koude buitenlucht -10°C

terugwinning van warmte,
vocht of koude uit de afvoerlucht

warme afzuiglucht +22°C   warme toevoerlucht +19°C

110°

1000L

16-18°C

OPTIE: waterbuffer voor warmteaccumulatie

ventilation to expel heat out the roof. Natural ventilation provides workers with exceptional thermal comfort year round. In the interior, a truly flexible work environment was achieved by using concrete floor slabs with an under-floor air distribution system that eliminated the need for a dropped ceiling and maximized the floor-to-floor dimension. A raised floor system also allowed for flexibility in arranging the individual offices and future expansion by using non-bearing partition walls. The building material choices were based on a full life-cycle cost analysis such as using sustainably harvested woods throughout. The building as a whole is a sophisticated functional office environment within a modern innovative skin.

PREVIOUS PAGE: A central atrium brings light into the core reception space. FSC-certified wood was used throughout.

TOP: The section illustrates the various sustainable strategies used throughout the design such as photovoltaic arrays, natural ventilation, and rainwater collection.

TOP: The semi-enclosed exterior space functions as an emergency escape, a maintenance corridor and outdoor terraces.

BOTTOM LEFT: The screens serve to reduce glare and filter direct and indirect daylight into the interior work spaces.

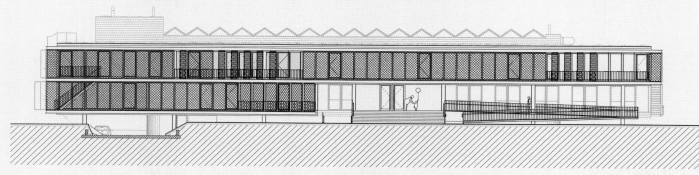

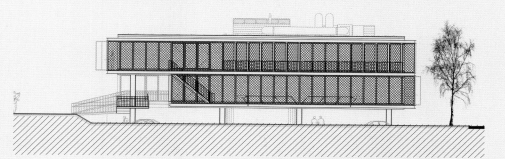

TOP LEFT: View of entrance to the building.

MIDDLE LEFT: North elevation.

BOTTOM LEFT: East elevation.

TOP RIGHT: Second-floor plan.

MIDDLE RIGHT: First-floor plan. All the offices are pushed to the exterior window walls to give every office views to the outdoors and access to optimal daylight.

BOTTOM RIGHT: Parking level plan. The structural column grid spacing was arrived at by using the width of three parked cars.

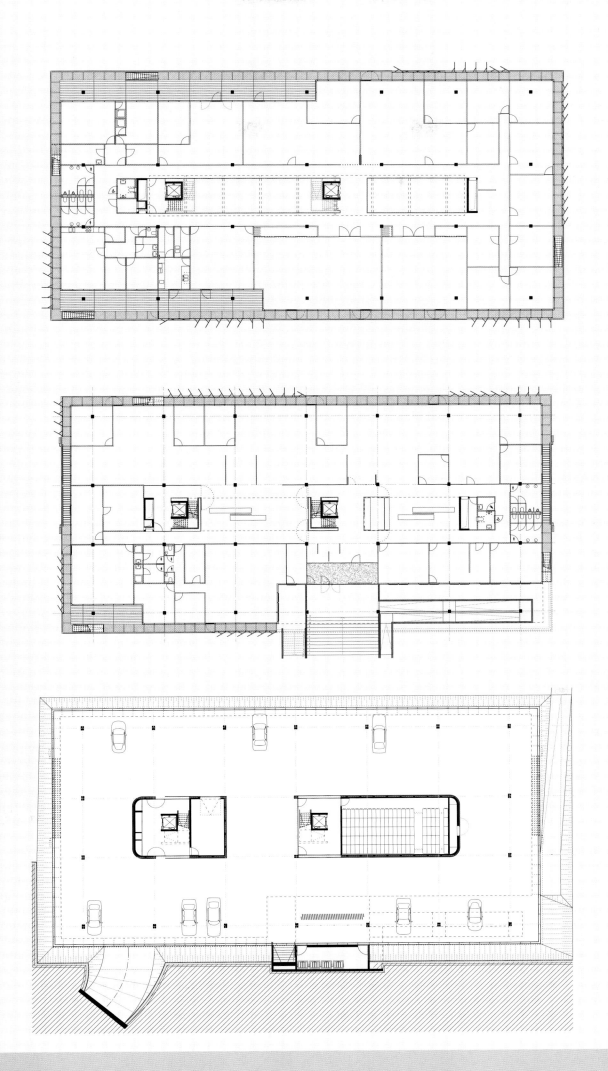

TOP: In the evening the building undergoes a transformation: the outer skin becomes almost invisible, the interior is revealed to the public outside.

LEFT: Building section through core. A raised two-story volume perched on concrete columns minimized excavation and foundation material that would have been used in traditional underground parking. It functions to provide open air and shaded parking for cars.

RIGHT: Exterior view of building during the day.

TOP LEFT: Galvanized steel screens provide sunshade while preserving views to the landscape.

BOTTOM LEFT: Close-up of pivoting galvanized screens.

RIGHT: A continuous galvanized steel mesh sunscreen wraps the entire building.

The Office of Olson Sundberg Kundig Allen

ARCHITECT: Olson Sundberg Kundig Allen Architects

AREA: 16,565 Square Feet

LOCATION: Seattle, Washington

PHOTOGRAPHERS: Benjamin Benschneider, Tim Bies

The historic rehabilitation of the Washington Shoe Building in the Pioneer Square Historic District in Seattle, Washington, demonstrates that going green can inspire cutting edge design. When Olson Sundberg Kundig Allen Architects moved from two locations in downtown Seattle it consolidated its office into one large studio to house a growing staff. Since the architects were their own client, they were able to experiment with new sustainable building materials and methodologies. Sustainable ideas were explored through the use of natural ventilation, by leaving the warehouse shell virtually untouched and by experimenting with materials such as masonite sheets for floors and unfinished steel. Instead of going to the landfill, the old staff workstations (made up of a series of painted modular cubes) were reused and incorporated into the new office design. The various sized cubes came together to form a large central cube that on the inside house a kitchenette and reprographic area. The outside of the cubes provides space for the office resource library.

    The original building had its ceiling skylights closed off years ago. To pay homage to the original use, one 6-ton, 14x25 foot counter-weighted skydoor was designed to bring light into the two levels of office space

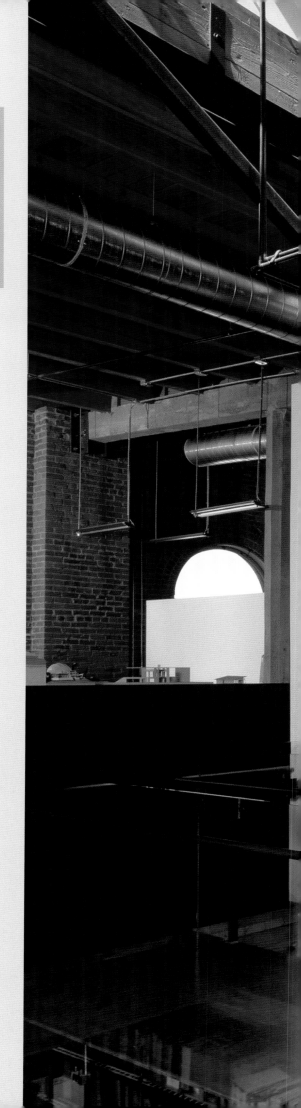

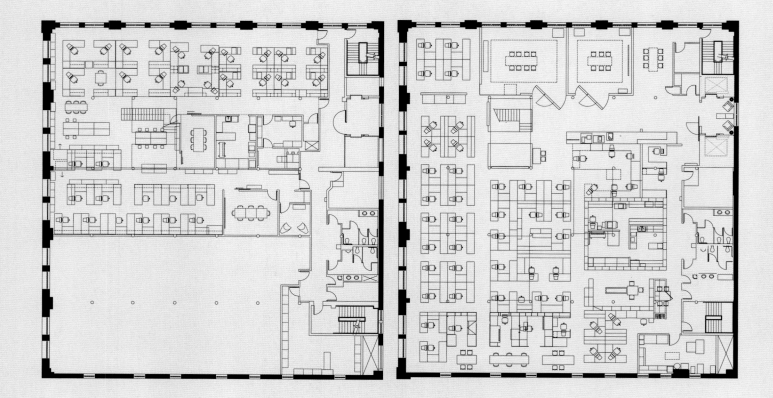

below. The steel skylight made of 90% recycled material (and recyclable forever), provides natural ventilation to the occupants. Inspired by a 19th century steam engine, the skydoor levers are controlled by two six foot blackened steel pistons which raise the door. Powered by only city water pressure, one valve draws water into a cylinder, forcing its piston up with the help of a 3-ton counterweight on the roof above. A second valve releases the water to lower the skylight. Twelve gallons of water that are forced through the hydraulic system are reclaimed and used to irrigate a roof garden.

The office plan layout pulls the workstations away from the perimeter walls to limit contact with the existing historic structure and to take advantage of better natural daylight, circulation paths through the office and to avoid the hierarchy associated with the "corner office." The architects experimental use of materials and inventive approach to design results in a vibrant work environment where creativity thrives.

PREVIOUS PAGE: A central stair sliced through the two levels exposing layers of century-old building materials.

TOP FAR LEFT: Fifth-floor plan.

TOP LEFT: Sixth-floor plan.

TOP RIGHT: The custom office workstations were all made of formaldehyde-free plywood and the use of pvc free carpet tiles were used in the office areas.

BOTTOM RIGHT: Experimental use of masonite for floors, walls and reception desk.

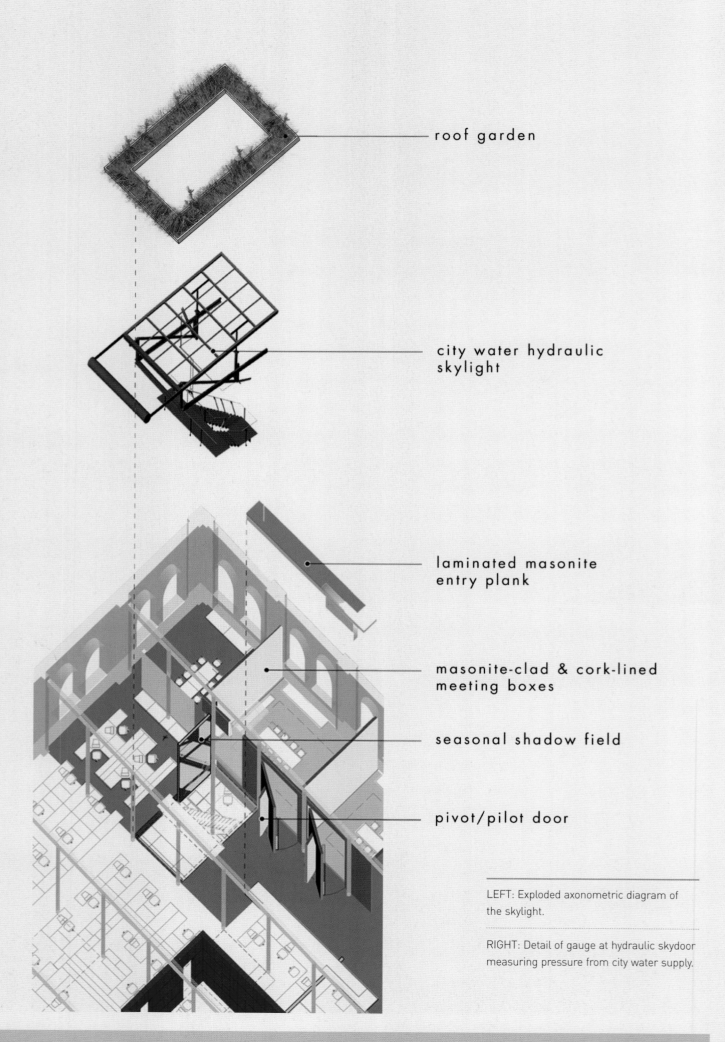

roof garden

city water hydraulic
skylight

laminated masonite
entry plank

masonite-clad & cork-lined
meeting boxes

seasonal shadow field

pivot/pilot door

LEFT: Exploded axonometric diagram of
the skylight.

RIGHT: Detail of gauge at hydraulic skydoor
measuring pressure from city water supply.

TOP LEFT: Detail of interlocking levers that operate skydoor above.

BOTTOM LEFT: Detail of hydraulic pistons at skydoor assembly.

TOP RIGHT: Cork walls clad the interior conference walls, ceilings and floor, for acoustic purpose and practical pin up space.

BOTTOM RIGHT: A relic of one gray furniture cube salvaged from the previous office furniture is left unfinished. The cubes grouped together have their second life as the office library storage shelves.

Jean Vollum Natural Capital Center

ARCHITECT: Holst Architecture + Soljaga Design Group

AREA: 70,000 Square Feet

LOCATION: Portland, Oregon

PHOTOGRAPHER: Holst Architecture & Dan Tyrpak

The rehabilitation of the Jean Vollum Natural Capital Center, in Portland's Pearl District, is the first restoration of a historic building in the nation to receive LEED Gold Certification. Instead of building a new structure, a warehouse built in 1895, was selected as a major part of the sustainable strategy. The majority of the original structure is retained and exposed, and the portion of the building that they were not able to renovate was used as salvage material for much of the building. The three-story building houses retail, commercial and office space. The facility was built to inspire its guests and tenants by displaying how real sustainable solutions can be found for building, even in the most tightly developed urban areas. In keeping with the spirit of the design, tenants are selected for their commitment to economic and environmental sustainable principles. This commitment extends to the community by offering the building's parking lot to be used for public markets and street fairs.

Recycled, salvaged or certified materials were used throughout the building. During construction, all by-products went through an aggressive recycling program which diverted an impressive 98% of the project's waste from the landfill. Through the use of energy-efficient windows, lighting fixtures, building controls and ventilation system, the building consumed 22% less energy than Oregon code.

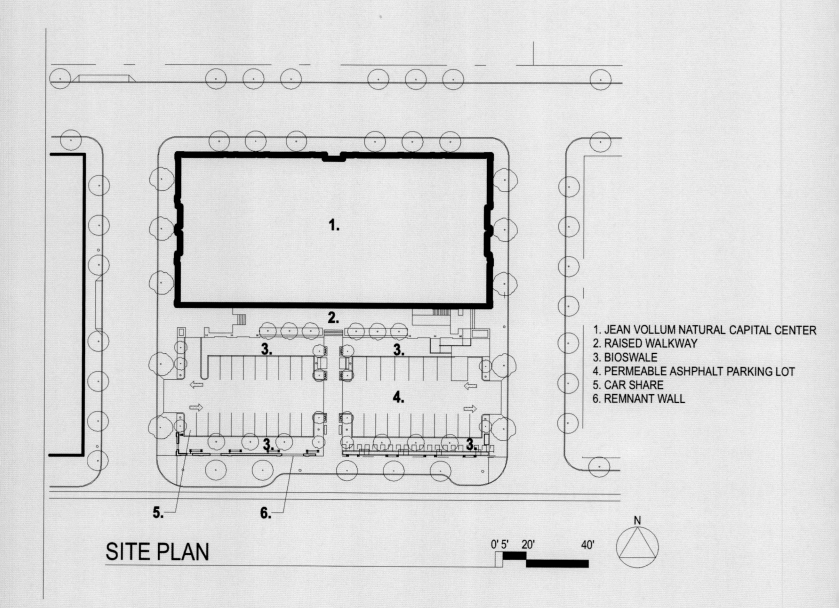

1. JEAN VOLLUM NATURAL CAPITAL CENTER
2. RAISED WALKWAY
3. BIOSWALE
4. PERMEABLE ASHPHALT PARKING LOT
5. CAR SHARE
6. REMNANT WALL

SITE PLAN

0' 5' 20'   40'

N

The Natural Capital Center poses no burden on Portland's stormwater drainage system because stormwater from the site is sent to a bioswale. A vegetated roof on the captures rainwater and any excess water that is not used by landscaping is then channeled to the bioswale. Beautiful landscape of native plants and trees are composed of drought tolerant species. The building has been recognized as a vital improvement to the City's landscape, and as a striking example of environmental innovation.

PREVIOUS PAGE: Interior view of the atrium and conference center. Structural wood timbers and original wood floor were refinished to maintain the character of the building. The existing brick walls and wood columns were blasted using ground corn-cobs and walnut shells.

TOP RIGHT: Third-level floor plan surrounded by a vegetated green roof.

MIDDLE UPPER RIGHT: Second-floor plan.

MIDDLE RIGHT: First-floor plan.

BOTTOM RIGHT: The site was chosen in part for its proximity to a wide variety of public transportation options to reduce demand of fossil fuel intensive transportation.

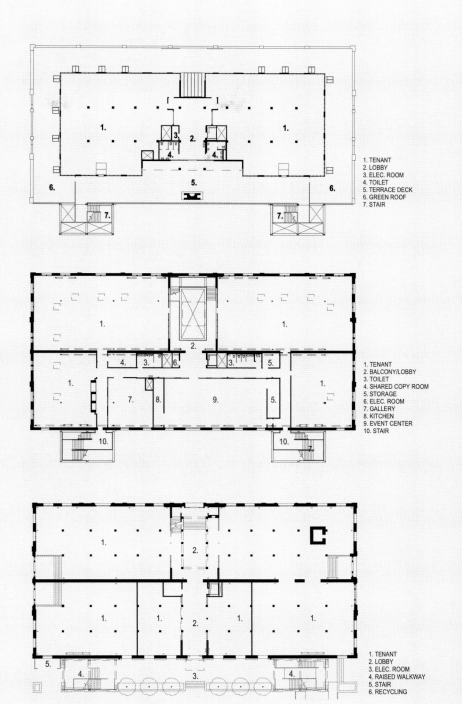

1. TENANT
2. LOBBY
3. ELEC. ROOM
4. TOILET
5. TERRACE DECK
6. GREEN ROOF
7. STAIR

1. TENANT
2. BALCONY/LOBBY
3. TOILET
4. SHARED COPY ROOM
5. STORAGE
6. ELEC. ROOM
7. GALLERY
8. KITCHEN
9. EVENT CENTER
10. STAIR

1. TENANT
2. LOBBY
3. ELEC. ROOM
4. RAISED WALKWAY
5. STAIR
6. RECYCLING

THE COVE

UPPER LEFT: Exposed brick walls, timber beams and large, arched openings and windows characterize the interior spaces.

BOTTOM LEFT: Recycled paint was used in the offices.

UPPER RIGHT: Meeting areas expose the original structure behind.

BOTTOM FAR RIGHT: FSC certified lumber is used in flooring, partitions, construction plywood, window frames and furniture.

BOTTOM RIGHT: Reception area.

TOP LEFT: The parking lot is used for markets and street fairs. Limited car parking along with proximity to several forms of mass-transit encourage occupants not to drive to work.

BOTTOM LEFT: Third floor rooftop terrace with outdoor fireplace.

UPPER RIGHT: Third floor lobby and entrance to deck. A majority of the materials used in the construction of the third floor were salvaged from the pre-existing structure.

LOWER RIGHT: Photo-sensors regulate control of the lights during the daytime.

Institute For Forestry and Nature Research (IBN)

■ ■

ARCHITECT: Behnisch Architekten

AREA: 122,195 Square Feet

LOCATION: Wageningen, Netherlands

PHOTOGRAPHER: Christian Kandzia, Martin Schodder

Native trees, bushes and grasses were planted in the environs of the IBN Institute's new building, providing a habitat—a home, protection, and peace—for staff members as well as for many plant and animal species. The Dutch Ministry of Agriculture, Nature, and Fishery and the Ministry for Housing Planning and Environment needed a new building for the Institute for Forestry and Nature Research (IBN) (now called Alterra) which consisted of three branches previously located in different buildings. The Ministry offered a site north of the university town of Wageningen, set in a region that was previously devastated by intensive agricultural use, polluted with fertilizers, and deprived of its natural elements. A careful analysis of the existing elements in the surrounding region led to an innovative interior and exterior landscape concept.

Glass roofs cover the gardens and connect the three buildings which are comprised of a library, conference center, and cafeteria. The large air volume within the covered atrium in conjunction with the vegetation naturally regulate temperatures in the winter and summer months. Cooling is achieved through evaporation of water by plants and pond surfaces. Heating is achieved through a greenhouse effect from the large glass enclosures. Materials such as unvarnished wood, concrete, glass

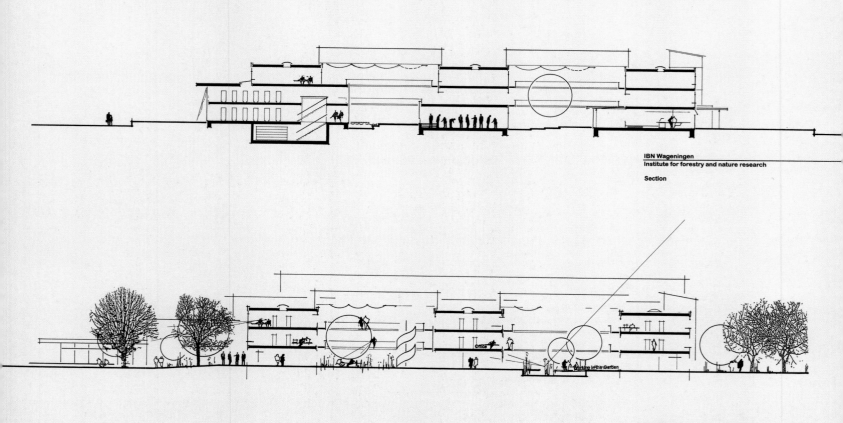

IBN Wageningen
Institute for forestry and nature research

Section

IBN Wageningen
Institute for forestry and nature research

Section

and galvanized steel were specified for their sustainable characteristics. Wherever human contact was abundant wood was specified for its low thermal conductivity and tactile qualities. On the exterior an environmentally conscious landscape concept was adopted that produced a greenbelt linking a nearby nature preserve to a nature conservancy on the Rhine river. This interconnected environment encourages more dialogue among researchers, which is in stark contrast to the conventional compartmentalized research communities. The resulting interior and exterior environments create a dynamic workplace coupled with nature.

PREVIOUS PAGE: The enclosed gardens and galleries encourage more interaction among researchers.

TOP: Site plan. An environmentally sound landscape concept was developed (with elements such as dry-stone walls, trees, hedges, berms, ponds, swamps, tree lanes, and water channels), producing a green belt linking a nearby nature reserve park in the east to the Rhine valleys in the west.

TOP RIGHT: Natural flora and fauna fill the covered courtyard interiors.

MIDDLE RIGHT: Cross Section through atrium.

BOTTOM RIGHT: Cross Section through atrium.

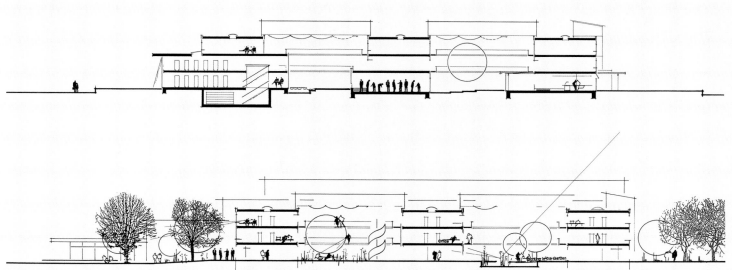

TOP LEFT: The transparent building allows daylight to flood into every corner of the interior through a double glazed roof.

BOTTOM LEFT: Unvarnished wood, concrete, galvanized steel, and clear glass were specified for their environmental and cost benefits.

TOP: Offices adjacent to the building's covered gardens (on higher levels) have a gallery for secondary routing, allowing workspaces to extend into the gardens.

RIGHT: The covered gardens offer alternative working or relaxation spaces.

The Smithsonian Tropical Research Institute

ARCHITECT: Kiss + Cathcart Architects

AREA: 15,000 Square Feet

LOCATION: Bocas del Toro, Republic of Panama

PHOTOGRAPHER: Kiss + Cathcart

A new research campus in Panama, located on a sensitive coastal site, is an example of how new construction can have minimal environmental impact. The Smithsonian Tropical Research Institute (STRI) is one of the world's leading centers for basic research on the ecology, behavior and evolution of tropical organisms. The building houses a laboratory for visiting and resident scientists to research the local marine biology environment. The laboratory building has 8,000 square feet of enclosed floor area and a further 7,000 square feet of exterior work areas and walkways.

Sustainable local hardwood was used for the columns, wall framing, cladding, doors, windows and the exposed roof structure. The roof with its large overhangs, shade interior volumes, lower solar heat gain and provide protected coverage from the rain that averages close to ten inches a month.

The narrow cross-section and raised floor slab maximize cross ventilation for cooling, and allows for daylight and views through the space. A long bridge extends across an existing pond on the site where a constructed wetland is planned to treat gray and black water waste in the future. Rainwater collected from the roof is filtered and used as the main water supply for the building. This treated water is stored in tanks that have a 3,000 gallon capacity.

PREVIOUS PAGE: View of North facade

LOWER RIGHT: Upper floor plan. The long linear plan with wrap around overhangs house laboratories, offices, conference rooms and a library.

TOP RIGHT: A long bridge extends to the building across an existing pond on the site where a constructed wetland is planned for the treatment of gray water waste in the future.

The roof is comprised of standard thin semi-transparent photovoltaic roof tiles, intermittent clear and a lower roof of translucent fiberglass sandwich panels that at night become visually animated with light. These photovoltaic arrays produce and supply most of the electrical requirements for the building. The climactic conditions of a tropical—hot and humid—location allowed for the design of the roof system to not require insulation. The transparency achieved in the roof allowed for diffused daylight to illuminate some of the work environments during the day. The building as a whole collects most of the energy needed to run the laboratory, collects the water it consumes, and it will treat all of its waste water (black and gray) with the constructed wetland which is currently being designed.

Upper Floor Plan

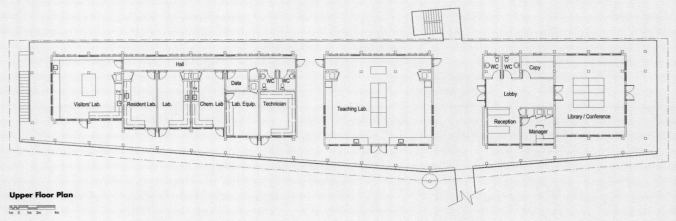

1m 0   1m 2m   4m

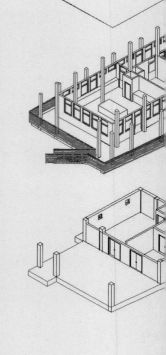

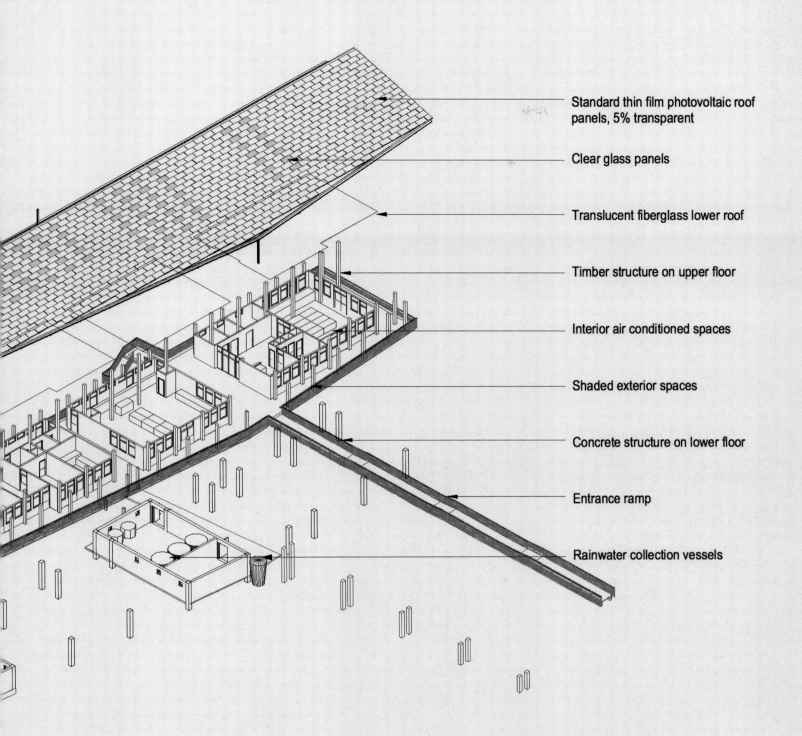

Standard thin film photovoltaic roof panels, 5% transparent

Clear glass panels

Translucent fiberglass lower roof

Timber structure on upper floor

Interior air conditioned spaces

Shaded exterior spaces

Concrete structure on lower floor

Entrance ramp

Rainwater collection vessels

TOP LEFT: Photovoltaic tiles replace conventional roof materials.

BOTTOM LEFT: Photovoltaic panels over exposed wood framing allow for minimal light transmission.

TOP RIGHT: Exploded axonometric.

BOTTOM RIGHT: Translucent ceiling panels in the workplace provides even interior illumination.

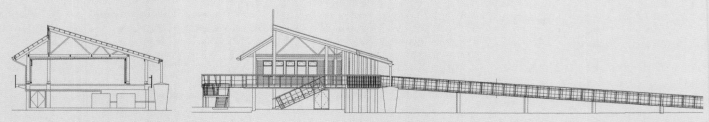

BOTTOM LEFT: Transverse section. Narrow cross section and raised floor slab to maximize cross ventilation for cooling.

TOP: At night the roof becomes animated with
the transparency of the roof tiles.

BOTTOM RIGHT: South elevation.

Lewis and Clark State Office Building

ARCHITECT: BNIM Architects

AREA: 120,000 Square Feet

LOCATION: Jefferson City, Missouri

PHOTOGRAPHERS: Mike Sinclair + Farshid Assassi

The Lewis and Clark State office building marks a new level of stewardship of the environment with a thoughtful reclamation of a highly neglected and damaged site. As part of its mission to protect and restore the states natural resources, the Missouri Department of Natural Resources commissioned a new office facility to showcase affordable sustainable strategies while achieving a LEED Platinum rating. A restorative site plan was designed, setting new standards for stormwater management, with the incorporation of bioswales and plantings to mitigate runoff.

Sustainable strategies were initiated even during the demolition phase of an existing prison complex on the site by diverting materials typically headed to the landfill for other uses. Some of the exterior landscaping features were made from bricks recovered from the site. Due to exceptional efforts made by the contractor, 88.6% of construction waste was diverted from the landfill to various locations laid out in a construction waste management plan. The building is designed to be 55% more efficient than a traditional building and will support 2.5% of this energy from photovoltaic panels integrated into the standing seam roof. Rainwater collected on the roof is stored in a 50,000 gallon tank, which provides flushing water to the

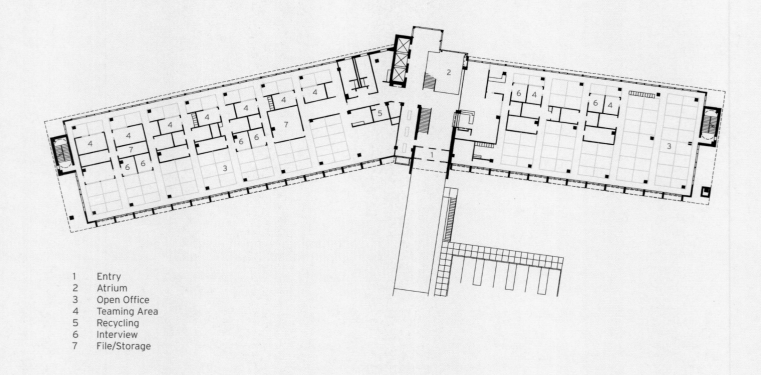

1   Entry
2   Atrium
3   Open Office
4   Teaming Area
5   Recycling
6   Interview
7   File/Storage

building toilets.

Each elevation was designed to respond to the varying climactic conditions. Ribbed precast concrete fins protruding four feet from the building's face were designed for the south facade and allow low-angled sun rays to provide supplemental heat during the cold winter months, yet block heat gain during the intense summer months. By contrast, the north facade was developed without shading devices, maximizing daylight and views toward the river. The long rectilinear wings and simple form allow for a flexible open plan. By locating the circulation space around the perimeter, the occupants enjoy natural light and extraordinary views throughout work day. Comparing the last two years of occupancy in their old locations and the first two years in the new building, the Department of Natural Resources has seen a 7.5% decrease in absenteeism in the Lewis and Clark building.

PREVIOUS PAGE: Horizontal sun shades on the south facade.

TOP LEFT: Floor plan. The building organization consists of two wings extending out from a central four-story atrium

TOP RIGHT: North facade designed without shading devices, maximizing daylight and views toward the river.

BOTTOM RIGHT: The building section conforms to the natural grading of the site, which slopes downward from north to south.

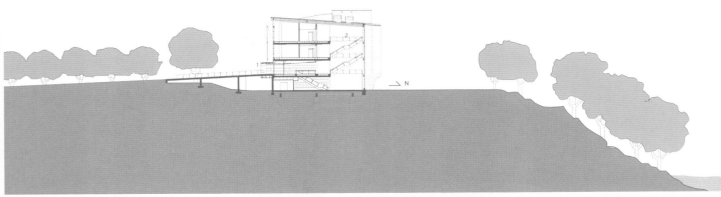

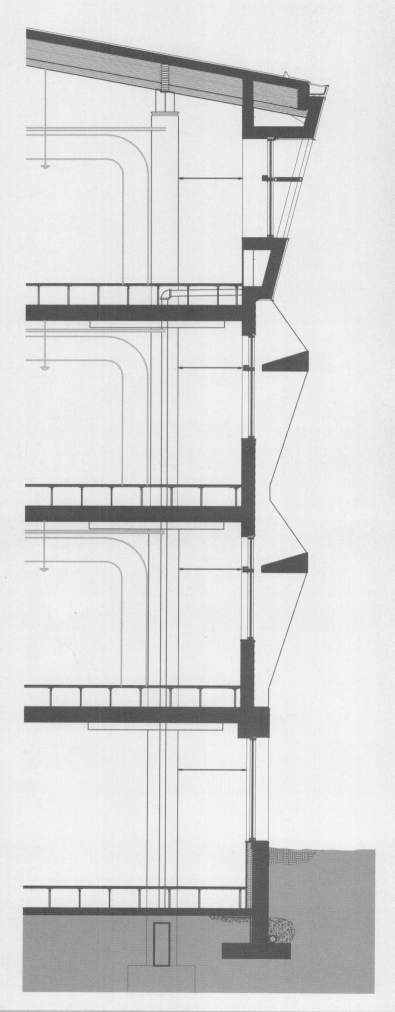

FAR LEFT: Wall section through ribbed facade and light shelves.

TOP LEFT: Close up of angled concrete fins.

TOP RIGHT: Different glazing was specifically selected for each elevation to maximize energy-efficiency.

BOTTOM RIGHT: Tinted glass was used on the south along with exterior sun shades. The placement of operable windows on all sides of the building allows for natural ventilation.

BOTTOM FAR RIGHT: Atrium circulation space faces north looking out toward the view of the river.

TOP LEFT: Work stations with low partitions walls to maximize daylight in building core .

BOTTOM FAR LEFT: On-site bike storage encourages people to commute using their bicycles.

BOTTOM MIDDLE LEFT: Illuminated back lit panels add interest to the reception area.

BOTTOM LEFT: To promote recycling a central collection system with chutes dedicated for paper and other recyclable products making it easy to use and collect.

RIGHT: By locating circulation space at the perimeter of the building, occupants are exposed to more natural light and extraordinary views.

Green Door

ARCHITECT: Envision Design

AREA: 16,500 Square Feet

LOCATION: Washington, District of Columbia

PHOTOGRAPHER: Michael Moran

The conversion of an aging warehouse not only recycled a building, but also afforded the opportunity to contribute to the revitalization of a transitional urban neighborhood. Constructed on a modest budget in 2003, Green Door houses the offices and day service programs for a non-profit community organization that prepares people with severe and persistent mental illness to work and live independently. Instead of building a new structure, the clients sought to impact minimally the environment by transforming a 1950s-era warehouse into a healthful environment for patrons and staff. Another goal was to reduce operating costs through energy-efficient design.

This incorporation of sustainable design concepts was central to the design of the facility. Very little demolition was required in the existing warehouse space due to the openness and lack of finishes. To increase the access to natural daylighting the building's perimeter window area was increased by 300% and four large skylights were added to the roof. This allowed 99% of the permanent workspaces to have access to natural light either from a window or skylight. By installing operable windows, employees benefit from fresh air when conditions outside permit.   Energy efficient strategies include insulating the entire space, providing low-

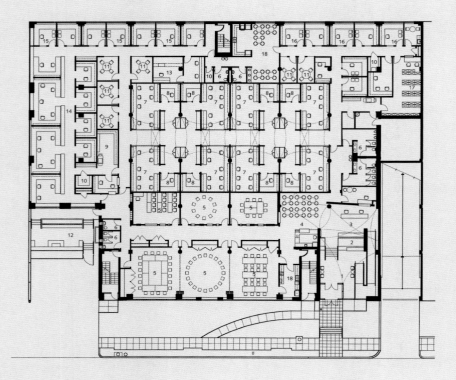

mercury fluorescent lamps throughout, selecting energy efficient appliances, and installing an efficient mechanical system that will pay for itself in seven years through reduced energy costs. Water use is reduced through low-flow plumbing fixtures. All work spaces are made from rapidly renewable and low-VOC emitting materials such as millwork made from strawboard panels, and FSC-certified woods. Even the employee's posture was taken into consideration, by providing ergonomic seating for all employees. The result is an energy efficient and environmentally responsible space that supports the organization's respect for the people they serve.

PREVIOUS PAGE: Main entrance to the converted 1950s warehouse.

TOP LEFT: Floor plan.

TOP RIGHT: A stretched fabric ceiling system disguises simple strip fluorescent light fixtures and diffuses the light from four large skylights that were cut into the roof above the central work areas.

RIGHT: A typical work space has file cabinets that were salvaged and refurbished.

TOP LEFT: Reception area.

BOTTOM LEFT: Reception area water feature.

RIGHT: Rapidly renewable materials that were incorporated throughout such as linoleum flooring and millwork made from strawboard panel products. Translucent panels in the hallway alcoves are made from recycled plastic.

ABOVE: Recycled materials that were used throughout the space include gypsum board (100%), ceiling panels (74%), ceramic tile (55%), and carpet (50%).. The cores of all wood doors are 100% Forest Stewardship Council Certified. All plywood and strawboard products are formaldehyde-free.

TOP RIGHT: Task chairs for employees that spend most of the day out of the office are salvaged and refurbished while full-day employees sit in new ergonomic task chairs that are 96% recyclable.

BOTTOM RIGHT: The break room painted with zero VOC paint in bright cheerful colors. Energy efficient low-mercury fluorescent lights were used throughout.

Environmental Science Building

■ ▪ ▪

ARCHITECT: Miller Hull Partnership

AREA: 58,500 Square Feet

LOCATION: Pierce County, Washington

PHOTOGRAPHER: Nic Lehoux, Pete Eckert

The Environmental Services Building is the first significant project to be built within the guidelines of the Chambers Creek Properties Master Plan, setting the tone for future development on the large site. The Pierce County Environmental Services Building is located on the 900+ acre Chambers Creek Properties in Washington, which includes 2½ miles of waterfront on Puget Sound. Much of the site has been actively and extensively mined for gravel for over 100 years, resulting in a barren landscape. Pierce County completed a 50-year Master Plan for the site focusing on "Reclaiming Our Resources," an effort that will gradually heal and rejuvenate the entire site by reintroducing native species and incorporating public uses. The local community was very active in the development of the Chambers Creek Properties Master Plan as well as in the development of this project. The Master Plan process received an American Planning Association Award for public involvement and won the AIA/COTE Top Ten Projects award for sustainable design. The owner partnered with various nonprofit organizations to promote interaction with the local community rather than for any economic benefit.

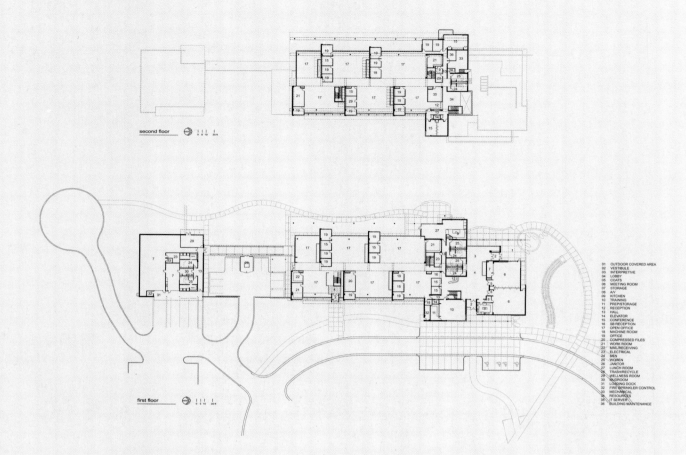

second floor

first floor

01 OUTDOOR COVERED AREA
02 VESTIBULE
03 INTERPRETIVE
04 LOBBY
05 COATS
06 MEETING ROOM
07 STORAGE
08 A/V
09 KITCHEN
10 TRAINING
11 PREP/STORAGE
12 RECEPTION
13 HALL
14 ELEVATOR
15 CONFERENCE
16 SB RECEPTION
17 OPEN OFFICE
18 MACHINE ROOM
19 OFFICE
20 COMPRESSED FILES
21 WORK ROOM
22 MAIL/RECEIVING
23 ELECTRICAL
24 MEN
25 WOMEN
26 JANITOR
27 LUNCH ROOM
28 TRASH/RECYCLE
29 WELLNESS ROOM
30 MUDROOM
31 LOADING DOCK
32 FIRE SPRINKLER CONTROL
33 MECHANICAL
34 RESOURCES
35 IT SERVER
36 BUILDING MAINTENANCE

The introduction of natural light, interior vegetation and views to the exterior make for a more humane work environment. Space planning was designed according to a European office model, where no desk is more than 30 feet to a window. Enclosed office pods containing the individual offices and conference rooms slash through the open office "tail" of the building and define the various departments while providing visual transparency through the structure. These office pods, or "chimneys," serve as the primary structure allowing the office interior to be virtually column-free. They also allow natural light, provide locations for interior planters, and are instrumental in the mechanical system design. A raised floor air distribution system reduces the size and energy consumption of the mechanical system, improves indoor air quality, provides for future flexibility, and gives individuals direct control of their immediate environment. The project attempts to make people aware of being part of a greater regional context by developing the "Rainier" axis through the site.

PREVIOUS PAGE: Main circulation stair brings light into two levels of office space.

TOP LEFT: Second-floor plan. Enclosed office pods containing the individual offices and conference rooms slash through the open office "tail" of the building and define the various departments while providing visual transparency through the structure.

BOTTOM LEFT: First-floor plan and site plan. The project attempts to make people aware of being part of a greater regional context by developing the "Rainier" axis through the site.

TOP RIGHT: Reception area and base of the vent wall system.

BOTTOM RIGHT: Exterior night view.

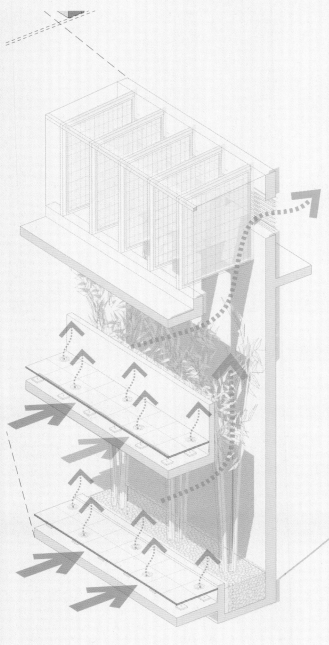

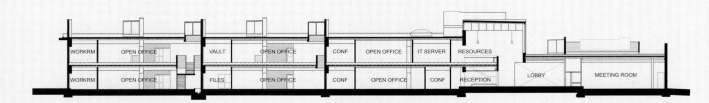

| WORKRM | OPEN OFFICE | | VAULT | OPEN OFFICE | | CONF | OPEN OFFICE | IT SERVER | RESOURCES | | | |
| WORKRM | OPEN OFFICE | | FILES | OPEN OFFICE | | CONF | OPEN OFFICE | CONF | RECEPTION | LOBBY | | MEETING ROOM |

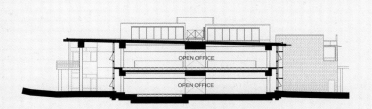

OPEN OFFICE

OPEN OFFICE

BOTTOM LEFT: Building cross section.

MIDDLE LEFT: Building longitudinal section.

TOP FAR LEFT: Introduction of natural light, interior vegetation and views to the exterior make for a more humane work environment.

TOP LEFT: Vent diagram.

TOP RIGHT: Space planning was designed according to a European office model, where no desk is more than 30 feet from a window.

TOP LEFT: Exterior view of full height window walls looking into the office space.

BOTTOM LEFT: Roof overhangs provide sun shading and minimize solar heat gain.

RIGHT: Sun shade devices diffuse light along the window walls.

Bückeburg Gas and Water Company

ARCHITECT: Randall Stout Architects

AREA: 18,138 Square Feet

LOCATION: Bückeburg, Germany

PHOTOGRAPHER: Peter Hübbe

The architect created a sustainable administration headquarters whose exterior quietly complemented the historic neighborhood and its interior conveyed 21st century functionality. Bückeburg Gas & Water Company, a city public works division responsible for water and natural gas distribution, is located in a 17th century castle town in Northern Germany. The moated castle itself is the central hub of a radial street pattern, which leads to civic buildings and sites, including a train station. The project responds to its urban context by providing a prominent front entry facing the train station. Between the two buildings, a 2½-story glass atrium serves as the project's circulation spine and the most prominent social space, encouraging staff interaction. The atrium unifies the new and existing small office blocks that reflect the scale of the adjacent residential neighborhood.

This building integrates energy-efficient components throughout, including photovoltaic panels that provide a substantial amount of electricity for lighting. In addition, solar hot water collectors are used to help provide domestic hot water for the building. These collectors also supply heat to the heat exchanger that is controlled by a building energy management system.

From the heat exchanger, warm air is pumped into tubes embedded in the concrete walls of the atrium stair, allowing it to serve as a thermal radiator for the atrium space. Atrium air warmed by the radiant heat is re-circulated through ducts on the atrium roof. The entire system can be reversed in summer months so that the thermal mass of the concrete stair walls act as a heat sink that removes heat from the atrium. Collectively, the sustainable principles applied in the design result in healthy, light-filled space, which have improved office morale, increased employee productivity and reduced absenteeism.

PREVIOUS PAGE: Atrium provides for natural daylighting and is designed for convection thermal exchange.

TOP LEFT: In respect to the surrounding historic district, the building's exterior was designed to be subtle and reserved, while the interior is dynamic and energetic.

TOP RIGHT: Ground-level floor plan.

MIDDLE RIGHT: Second-floor plan showing management and conference areas.

BOTTOM RIGHT: Third-floor plan showing mechanical rooms and light well.

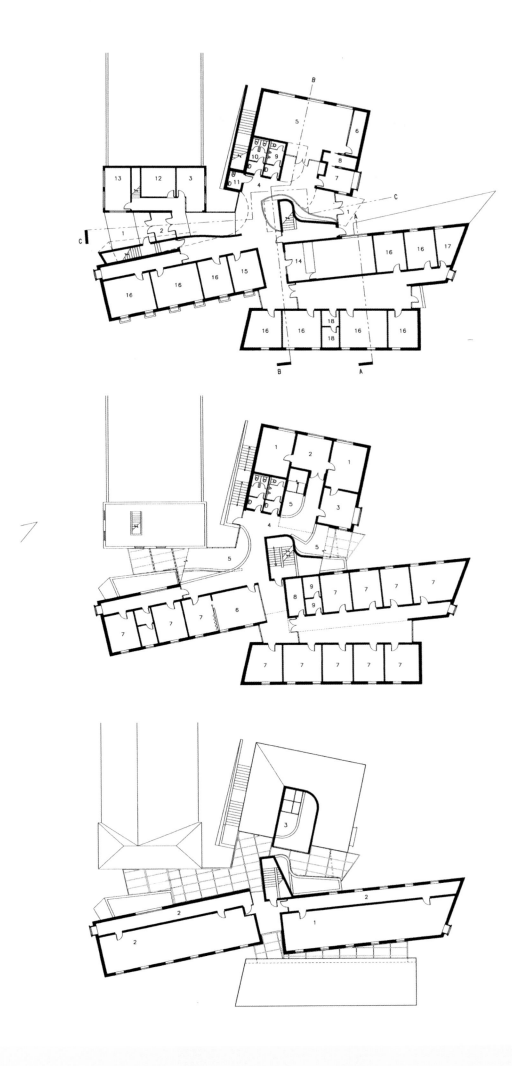

TOP LEFT: The entry creates a dialogue between traditional and contemporary forms.

BOTTOM LEFT: Energy diagram of the ventilation system with solar collector and absorption cooling.

TOP RIGHT: The project materials reflect some of the region's most prevalent materials: limestone and plaster.

MIDDLE RIGHT: A heat exchange system in mechanical room convert solar power into energy for building use.

LOWER RIGHT: Photovoltaic panels provide a substantial amount of electricity for lighting.

Bückeburg Gas & Water Company
Functional diagram of the ventilation system with solar collector, and absorption cooling.

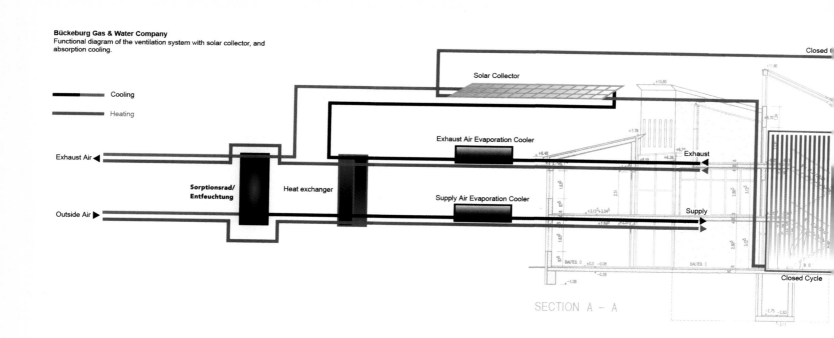

Cooling

Heating

Solar Collector

Closed Cycle

Exhaust Air Evaporation Cooler

Exhaust Air ◄

Exhaust ►

Sorptionsrad/ Entfeuchtung

Heat exchanger

Supply Air Evaporation Cooler

Outside Air ►

Supply ►

Closed Cycle

SECTION A - A

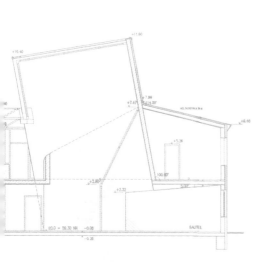

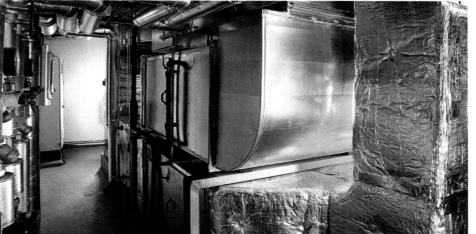

TOP LEFT: Interior office work station.

BOTTOM LEFT: Based on the company's work with water and natural gas, the architects designed circulation spaces that echo the movement of water and gas, to staff and visitors.

TOP RIGHT: Staff entry vestibule.with a 2½-story glass atrium serves as the project's circulation spine.

BOTTOM RIGHT: Skylight above conference room entry.

Greenpeace USA Headquarters

ARCHITECT: Envision Design

AREA: 17,400 Square Feet

LOCATION: Washington, District of Columbia.

PHOTOGRAPHER: Michael Moran

Renowned for their activist commitment to solving global environmental problems, Greenpeace chose to incorporate this philosophy into the design of their new headquarters. The choice of an urban site showcases how sustainable design solutions can be integrated on many scales. From the planning stages it was determined that the office structure would switch from enclosed offices to an entirely open plan at all levels of the organization. The decision to build out a space with no enclosed offices helped increase the design efficiency of the space in many ways. Walls parallel to the perimeter windows were kept low, to allow as much natural light as possible into the space. Open workstations placed at the perimeter of the building, allow as much natural light as possible into the individual workstations. Less commonly used support functions were placed in a central location on the interior. Enclosed huddle rooms are placed throughout the space to allow for confidential meetings and enclosed booths were provided for private telephone conversations. Adjacent to the reception area is a flexible main conference room with the capability of opening up to the adjoining areas for large staff meetings and receptions. A large break room was designed to further promote staff interaction.

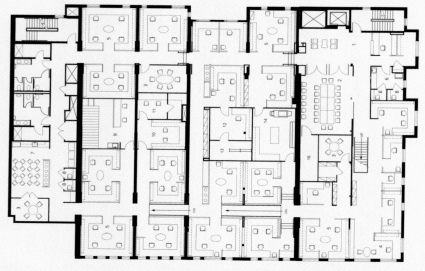

1 RECEPTION
2 CONFERENCE ROOM
3 HUDDLE AREA
4 DIRECTOR
5 WORK STATION
6 PANTRY
7 BREAK ROOM
8 PHONE BOOTH
9 ARCHIVES
10 PHOTO WORKROOM
11 EDIT SUITE
12 M.I.S. WORKROOM
13 COMPUTER ROOM
14 COPY ROOM
15 LIBRARY
16 ELECTRICAL
17 LIGHT WELL

In order to maximize space efficiency in the existing irregular space, custom workstations were designed for each area. Both a wheatboard and Forest Stewardship Council (FSC) certified particleboard were used as primary materials. Even the conference room chairs use sustainable fabrics on wooden shells sourced from well-managed forests. Zero or low VOC coatings and adhesives were used throughout. It was decided that both the space and the base building would be PVC free (PVC is known to be one of the most toxic building materials on the market today). A commitment was also made to employ both photovoltaic and thermal panels on the roof of the building to supplement electric power and hot water requirements. The Greenpeace headquarters showcases the rigorous and resourceful application of sustainable building techniques from its countertops made of recycled yogurt containers to the state-of-the-art mechanical systems.

PREVIOUS PAGE: For the reception area furniture, classic modern chairs made from cotton webbing on solid wood frames were special ordered to be fabricated from FSC certified maple.

TOP FAR LEFT: Third-floor plan.

TOP LEFT: Fourth-floor plan.

TOP RIGHT: In order to maximize space efficiency in the existing irregular space, custom workstations were designed for each area.

BOTTOM RIGHT: Refurbished high-end file cabinets were used throughout the space. Existing file cabinets were disassembled and repainted with a water-based paint then reassembled and rekeyed.

LEFT: The structural components of the stair are made from steel that contains over 96% recycled content.

TOP RIGHT: Reclaimed wood flooring was chosen for its durability and used on stair treads. Drywall ceilings with recessed fluorescent downlight fixtures are set at 8'-0" above the finished floor, which allowed the organization of ductwork, power, and data cabling above.

BOTTOM RIGHT: Other special millwork items included a large sliding wall made from wheatboard panels, glass and steel that separate the main conference room from an adjacent corridor. When in the open position, the effective space of the conference room is increased by 50%.

TOP LEFT: A series of oversized wheat board pivot doors separate the other side of the conference room to accommodate staff meetings for all 95 employees as well as large receptions.

BOTTOM LEFT: Exterior view of the historic brick building at dusk. The building is located directly across the street from an underground metro rail station and bus stops are outside the main building entrance encouraging use of public transportation.

RIGHT: A recycling station is centrally located in the break room to promote use. Cabinetry items in the break room and support areas were also built from wheatboard. An extremely durable solid surfacing material made from recycled yogurt containers serve as countertops.

The Gordon & Betty Moore Foundation

ARCHITECT: Gensler

AREA: 34,000 Square Feet

LOCATION: San Francisco, California

PHOTOGRAPHER: Chris Barrett

The Gordon and Betty Moore Foundation, a private philanthropic organization, transformed a 19th-Century military structure into their headquarters. This former military base (now a national park in San Francisco's Presidio) proved to be the ideal size for the new offices. The project combines concepts of a highly collaborative work culture with a profound commitment to sustainable design principles and processes.

The design incorporates a variety of work settings, project rooms and meeting spaces for just over one-hundred employees. The space embraces the foundation's sustainable principles of the foundation through the use of an open floor plan design and the creative reuse of existing and salvaged materials. These materials, many from local sources and materials found on the site, make up much of the constructed spaces, key furnishings and decorative display alcoves. Bricks from homes damaged by the Loma Prieta 1989 earthquake, wind fallen trees, and salvaged windows and doors are re-purposed and given new lives as partitions, stairs and furniture. These natural elements were balanced by an investment in technology, enabling a healthy and productive office environment.

PREVIOUS PAGE: Reception area showcases the alcove wall constructed with salvaged wood and steel.

TOP: This conference table was hewn from a bay laurel tree that was found near the site. The conference room door is made from wood debris found on the site.

TOP RIGHT: Third-floor plan.

MIDDLE RIGHT: Second-floor plan.

BOTTOM RIGHT: First-floor plan. The symmetrical plan of the 34,000 sq ft office in an existing military structure.

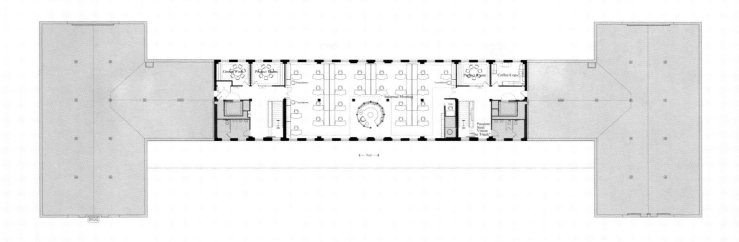

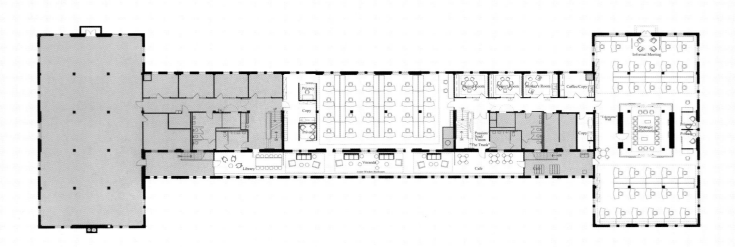

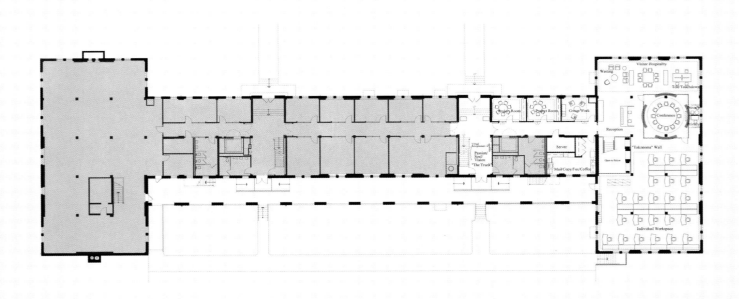

LEFT: Reclaimed wood from an old barn was used to clad the walls of the conference room and alcoves.

RIGHT: Sustainably grown materials like hemp are used in window shades that diffuse light into the space.

TOP LEFT: Workstations were made with certified woods.

BOTTOM FAR LEFT: Second-floor focus rooms framed in salvaged materials.

MIDDLE LEFT: Interior view of focus room.

RIGHT: Stair treads are made from wood from an old tree that was downed in the area.

Sedgwick Rd

■

ARCHITECT: Olson Sundberg Kundig Allen Architects
AREA: 33,000 Square Feet
LOCATION: Seattle, Washington
PHOTOGRAPHERS: Marco Prozzo, Tim Bies, Hans Fonk

-

The Old Star Machinery building on the edge of downtown Seattle demonstrates how salvaged and found materials can be used to create innovative and creative work environments. The Seattle subsidiary of the New York based advertising agency McCann Erikson moved and renamed itself as Sedgwick Rd. The agency sought to invest in a new space that reflects a collaborative environment that fosters creativity. The Star machinery building was rehabilitated by reusing building materials found on site. The existing structure was piled high with discarded beams, steel, and old windows and doors intended for the landfill. The effort to salvage as many materials found on site and integrate them into the design shifted the conventional thought on what is valuable. The large old windows and doors were stitched together to become movable conference room partitions. The resulting structure was nicknamed, "Frankenstein."

Additional sustainable strategies were to leave the shell of the structure untouched and the clerestory windows and scissor trusses raw and unpainted. Recycled steel was used for flooring, and stairs. Modular carpet tiling of recycled material was used in high traffic work areas. Former tool rooms on the shop's south side became house editing rooms,

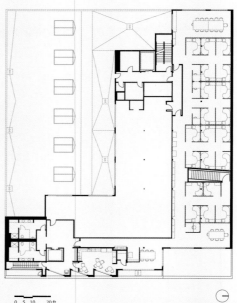

meeting areas, a library and a bar for office events. These rooms are tucked under a low ceiling have individual oversized doors that can be left open to the larger office space. This inventive office space breaks down barriers among the agency's creative, media and branding teams and results in a successful collaborative work environment.

PREVIOUS PAGE: Salvaged windows and steel doors form moveable partitions that make up the conference areas.

TOP LEFT: Exterior street view of the historic Star Machinery Building prior to renovation.

MIDDLE FAR LEFT: Second-floor plan.

MIDDLE: Third-floor plan.

MIDDLE SPINE: Fourth-floor plan.

TOP RIGHT: Original piles of debris were reused in the final design.

BOTTOM RIGHT: View of "Frankenstein" from the second level.

PREVIOUS PAGE: Existing trusses are left raw and unpainted, while new steel stair (which is 100% recyclable) and steel floor panels are in keeping with the industrial quality of the space.

LEFT: One configuration of flexible conference area nicknamed "Frankenstein."

TOP RIGHT: Former tool rooms on the shop's south side now house editing rooms.

BOTTOM RIGHT: Reception desk made from a salvaged steel I-beam.

Aspect Communications World Headquarters

ARCHITECT: McDonough + Partners

AREA: 110,000 Square Feet

LOCATION: San Jose, California

PHOTOGRAPHER: Steve Whittaker

Building sustainably sends the message that building green is good business. Aspect Communications Corporation is a leading provider of services that enable businesses to manage and optimize customer communications. The goal for the corporate headquarters expansion was to transformation a conventional office building into a sustainable work environment. The building houses offices, a corporate training center, and amenities, creating an urban setting that honors both people and the surrounding environment. The building has earned both an Award for Excellence in Architecture and a Presidential Citation for Sustainable Design.

The design promotes the occupants' health and well-being through the use of healthy building materials and by providing abundant access to fresh air and daylight. An under-floor air distribution system is utilized to give flexibility the open-floor plan while providing fresh air closer to the work areas. High floor-to-ceiling dimensions and narrow floor depths along with operable windows enhances indoor air quality and maximizes natural daylight. By leaving the structure exposed, off-gassing fireproof coatings are eliminated.

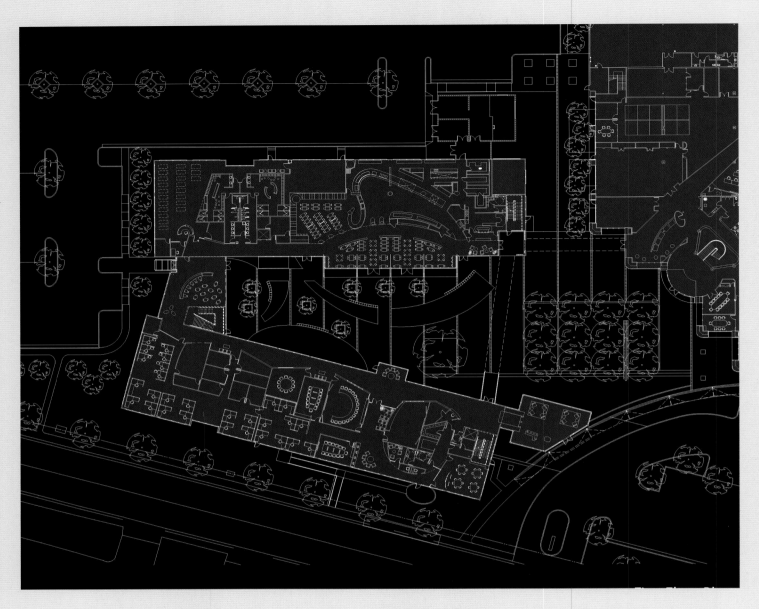

The integration of sustainable strategies is extended to the landscape as well, with a sophisticated water conservation strategy. A vegetation filled outdoor courtyard and reflecting pool provide a pleasant exterior space for both visitors and employees to enjoy. The reflecting pool and runnel is designed to accommodate transformation into a more natural wetland system in the future. The design for the headquarters is evidence that existing energy intensive buildings can transform into the ecologically intelligent buildings of the future.

PREVIOUS PAGE: Exterior view of reflecting pool.

TOP LEFT: Site plan.

TOP RIGHT: View of central courtyard.

BOTTOM RIGHT: Building section.

TOP LEFT: Exterior view of entrance to building.

BOTTOM FAR LEFT: Conference rooms into the courtyard.

BOTTOM LEFT: Balconies allow for a direct access to the outdoors.

TOP RIGHT: The design reinforces employees' connection to the outdoors, providing access to daylight, fresh air, and views throughout the building.

BOTTOM RIGHT: Communal lunch areas encourage communication and staff interaction.

Carnegie Institution for Science

DEPARTMENT OF GLOBAL ECOLOGY

ARCHITECT: EHDD Architecture

AREA: 11,000 Square Feet

LOCATION: Stanford, California

PHOTOGRAPHER: Peter Aaron & Paul Sterbentz

An unusual energy efficient mechanical system acts as the form generator for one of Stanford University's newest buildings. The design engineers used a unique "Night Sky" cooling system to address the extreme cooling loads inherent to the region. This ingenious system allowed for the elimination of traditional cooling equipment normally needed to condition a space of this size. Composed of a series of small exterior sprinklers this system sprays the roof at night with a thin film of water. The cooled water from the night air runs down the roof and is collected in storage tanks for cooling the building the next day. By not having to mechanically cool this water the building significantly saves on its energy costs.

The building features a uniquely designed cooling tower that is oriented to take advantage of the prevailing winds to catch breezes and direct this fresh air into the building. When natural breezes are absent, a spray ring within the tower evaporatively cools air creating a downdraft that carries cool air into the building.

The laboratory areas were zoned separately from the offices because of different ventilation requirements. The second floor offices are entirely naturally ventilated, which combined with radiant slab heating and cooling,

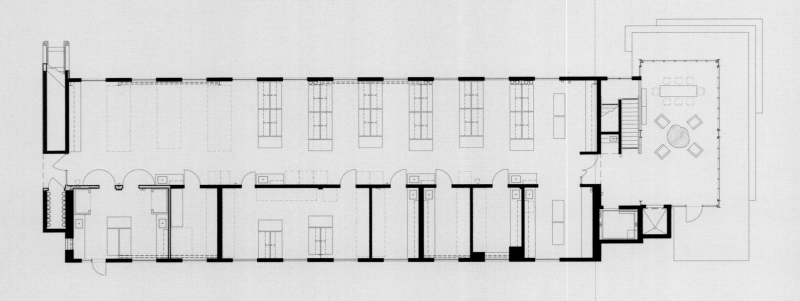

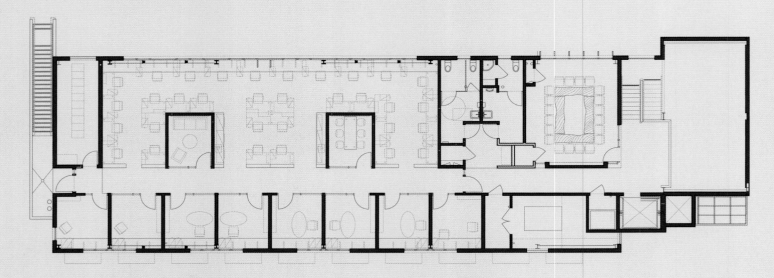

eliminates the need for traditional forced air ducting. The open lab plan and the radiant floor plan help distribute heat evenly through the upper levels. The expression and accessibility of the mechanical systems allows for the building to become a learning tool to promote a greater understanding of sustainably designed mechanical systems.

PREVIOUS PAGE: Main building at night.

TOP LEFT: Second-floor plan.

BOTTOM LEFT: First-floor plan.

TOP RIGHT: Southwest facade.

BOTTOM RIGHT: Southeast facade.

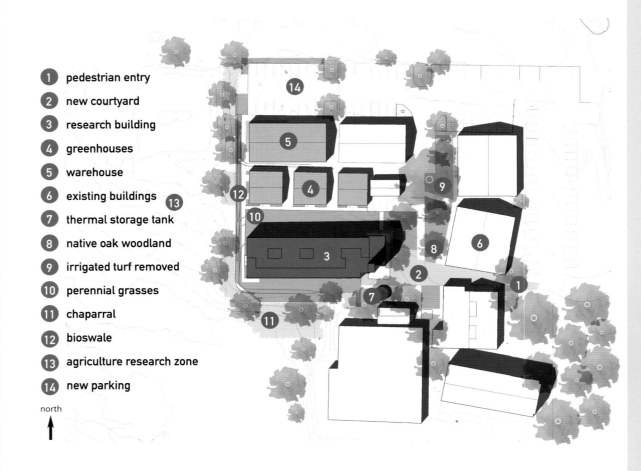

1. pedestrian entry
2. new courtyard
3. research building
4. greenhouses
5. warehouse
6. existing buildings
7. thermal storage tank
8. native oak woodland
9. irrigated turf removed
10. perennial grasses
11. chaparral
12. bioswale
13. agriculture research zone
14. new parking

north

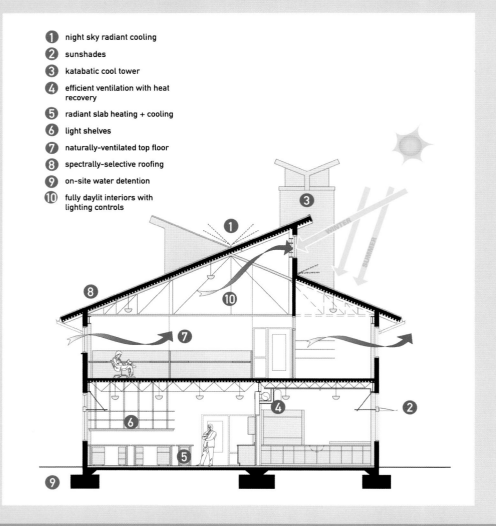

1. night sky radiant cooling
2. sunshades
3. katabatic cool tower
4. efficient ventilation with heat recovery
5. radiant slab heating + cooling
6. light shelves
7. naturally-ventilated top floor
8. spectrally-selective roofing
9. on-site water detention
10. fully daylit interiors with lighting controls

TOP LEFT: Site Plan.

BOTTOM LEFT: Cooling diagram.

TOP RIGHT: Roof sprinklers shown activated.

BOTTOM RIGHT: "Night Sky" radiant cooling diagram.

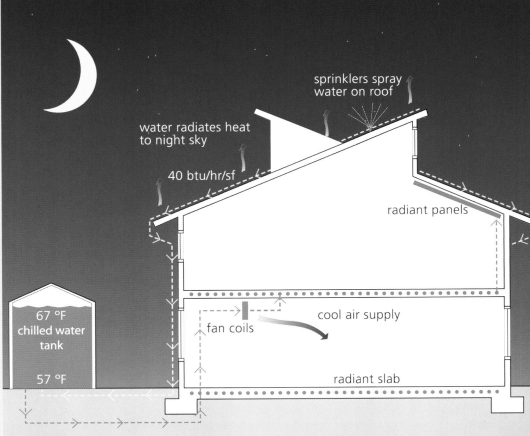

sprinklers spray
water on roof

water radiates heat
to night sky

40 btu/hr/sf

radiant panels

67 °F
chilled water
tank

57 °F

fan coils

cool air supply

radiant slab

LEFT: Operable clerestories allow for passive cooling.

TOP RIGHT: Open lab plans allow for maximum flexibility.

BOTTOM RIGHT: The staff lounge area has large opperable doors that enable a direct connection to the exterior.

The New York Times Building

ARCHITECT: Renzo Piano Building Workshop

FXFOWLE Architects

INTERIOR ARCHITECT: Gensler

AREA: 750,000 Square Feet

LOCATION: New York, New York

PHOTOGRAPHER: Nic Lehoux

The new headquarters for The New York Times Company is a flexible, environmentally sustainable workplace designed to support and foster innovations for this 21st century media company. The recently completed offices occupy 22 floors within the new 52 story office tower located in the heart of New York City. Gensler was hired to collaborate with the Times Company, the base building architects Renzo Piano Building Workshop and FXFOWLE architects to create a modern sustainable office environment. With unusually active involvement by the Owner's team, designers researched and implemented cutting-edge building technologies such as a sophisticated exterior ceramic sunscreen that deflects unwanted sunlight to reduce heat gain and a fully dynamic lighting system where shades automatically drop to block glare and the computer-controlled lights automatically adjust to take advantage of the sunlight.

The concept of layering and transparency are central to the office design. The open floor plan, with low partition walls, allows employees to work in a daylight-filled workplace. The enclosed rooms have glass partition walls to allow daylight to penetrate in and through the rooms while allowing privacy. Color is as an organizing principle that delineates various

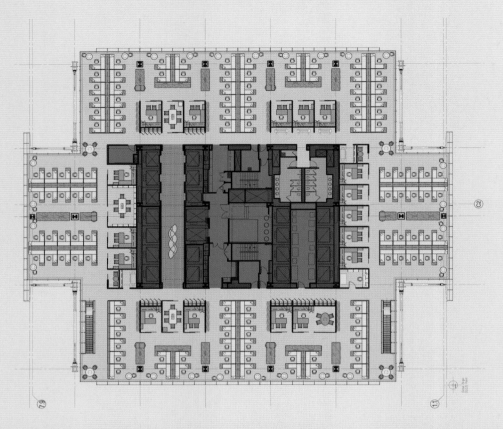

programmatic areas. Red is emphasized at the core and stair, green accents the offices, and blue defines the open plan areas.

Understanding the way in which the employees use their work space drove the design of the individual workstations. The work areas were ergonomically tailored to the writing-intensive needs of the staff, by putting the keyboard tray beneath the work surface and by specifying chairs that promote proper posture. The design team learned that reporters and editors were "pilers, not filers" who need easy access to research and source materials, and so adapted the design of custom workstations to maximize horizontal work surfaces and bookshelves. Like a New York City apartment, they utilize every square inch of the space from file cabinets that pull out to double as added seating, to a spine that is a floor to ledge bookshelf.

An under-floor air distribution system allows for flexible office configurations, flexible cable management, and energy efficient air distribution. Interior materials and finishes were selected in keeping with Piano's clean minimalism, using classic modern furnishings and natural materials. The rigorously calibrated building resonates with transparency and elegant simplicity inside and out.

PREVIOUS PAGE: Standing 856 feet high, the building is the first high-rise in the United States that utilizes a ceramic sunscreen.

LEFT: Color is used as an organizing principle throughout the space.

RIGHT: Axonometric of the office layout that shows the maximization of sunlight through the cruciform shape of the building and the shifting of closed offices to the core.

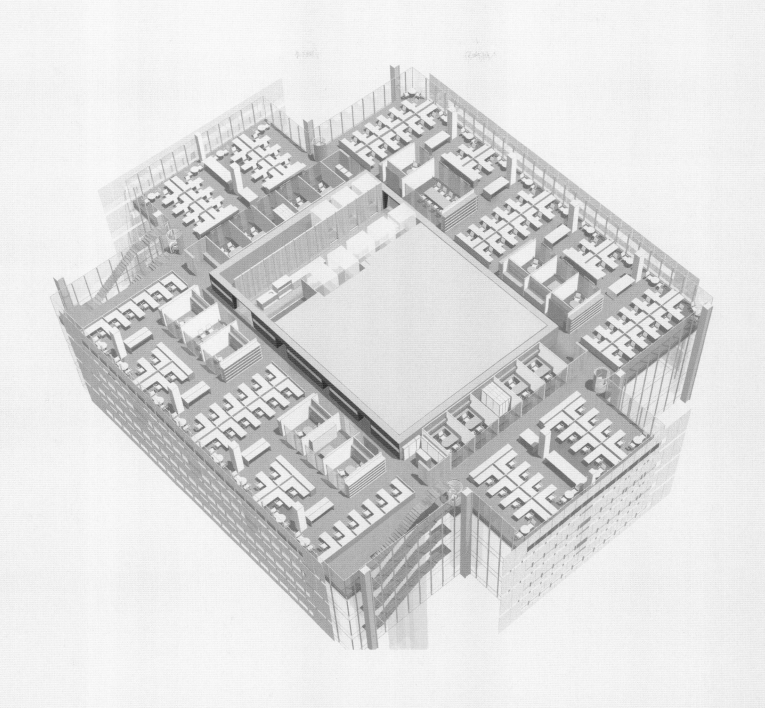

LEFT: Renzo Piano Building Workshop developed the design concept for two sets of interior stairs that occupy "pride of place" in the Western-facing corner's of the bulding. The open stairs with broad City views invite employees to move through the space, and animate the building for passersby.

TOP RIGHT: Daylight penetrates the entire space due to custom designed glass-fronted offices and partitions.

BOTTOM RIGHT: Low workstation panels, strategic circulation plans, and communicating stairs positioned on the perimeter all support the Times Company goal for a vibrant, stimulating workplace emphasizing strong communication, collaboration, and innovation.

TOP LEFT: Custom workstations were tailored for special needs of staff.

RIGHT: The employee cafeteria, with spectacular views, abundant natural light and an intimate connection with the City, is designed to invite informal meetings throughout the day

Directory

Chesapeake Bay Foundation
Phillip Merrill Environmental Center

Architect: Smith Group

500 Griswold - Suite 1700

Detroit, MI 48226

T: 313.983.3600

www.smithgroup.com

Client: Chesapeake Bay Foundation

Genzyme Center

Architect: Behnisch Architects, Inc.

344 Bolyston Street

Boston, MA 02116

T: 617.375.9380

www.behnisch.com

Design Architects Building and Interior: Behnisch

Architekten, Stuttgart, Germany

General Contractor: HITT Contracting, Inc.

Environmental Consultancy: Buro Happold, Bath (GB)

and New York, NY, Tony McLaughlin

Structural Engineer: Buro Happold, New York

M/E/P Engineer: Buro Happold, New York

Herman Miller International UK Headquarters

Architect: Gensler

33 Aldgate High Street

London, UK EC3N 1AH

T: 44 (0) 20 7073 9600

www.gensler.com

Client: Herman Miller

General Contractor: Hitt Contracting, Inc.

Construction Manager: Mark G. Anderson Consultants

MEP Engineer: GHT, Ltd.

Kitsap County Administration Building

Architect: Miller/ Hull Partnership, LLP

Polson Building

71 Columbia - Sixth Floor

Seattle, Washington 98104

T: 206.682.6837

www.millerhull.com

Client: The County of Kitsap, Washington

General Contractor: Swinerton Builders

Structural Engineer: AHBL

M/E/P Engineer: Abacus

Civil Engineer: SvR

Landscape Consultant: Site Workshop

Save The Bay Educational Center

Architect: Croxton Collaborative Architects

475 5th Avenue

New York, New York 10017

T: 212.683.1998

www.croxtonarc.com

Client: Save The Bay, Inc.

General Contractor: Agostini Construction

Environmental Consultancy: Andropogon Associates, Ltd.

Structural Engineer: Yoder & Tidwell

M/E/P Engineer: Lehr Consultants International

Civil Engineer: NorthEast Engineers

Landscape Consultant: Jose Alminana

SC3

Architect: Smith Carter Architects and Engineers Incorporated

1600 Buffalo Place

Winnipeg, MB

R3T 6B8

T: 204.477.1260

www.smithcarter.com

Client: Smith Carter Architects and Engineers Incorporated

General Contractor: MD Steele Construction Ltd.

Engineers: Smith Carter Architects and Engineers

Incorporated

Landscape Consultant: Smith Carter Architects and Engineers

Incorporated

Electrical Engineer: Flack + Kurtz

Mechanical Engineer: Flack + Kurtz

901 Cherry, Offices for Gap Inc.

Architect: William McDonough + Partners

700 East Jefferson Street

Charlottesvile, VA 22902

T: 434.979.1111

www.mcdonough.com

Client: GAP

Architects of Record: Rich Graziano & David Lehrer

Interior Architect: Gensler

General Contractor:

Environmental Consultancy:

Kresge Foundation Headquarters

Architect: Valerio Dewalt Train Associates

668 High Street

Palo Alto, CA 94301

T: 650.561.7000

www.buildordie.com

Client: The Kresge Foundation

Environmental Consultancy: Vinci-Hamp Architects +

Farr Associates

Structural Engineer: Robert Darvas Associates

M/E/P Engineer: Arup

Civil Engineer: Vinci-Hamp Architects

Landscape Consultant: Conservation Design Forum

Landscape Consultant: Site Workshop

Directory

Natural Resources Defense Council

Architect: Leddy Maytum Stacy Architects

677 Harrison Street

San Francisco, CA 94107

T: 415.495.1700

www.lmsarch.com

Client: Natural Resources Defense Council

Landscape Consultant: Site Workshop

City of White Rock Operations Building

Architect: Busby Perkins + Will

1220 Homer Street

Vancouver, B.C. V6B 2Y5

T: 604.689.5446

www.busby.ca

Client: The City of White Rock, British Columbia

Administrative Centre for the City of Bonheiden

Architect: VBM Architecten (Van Broeck & Meuwissen)

Now Lava Architecten & Bogdan and Van Broek Architects

Lava Architecten cvba

Parijsstraat 74

3000 Leuven A

T: 32 [0]16 23 01 41

www.lav-a.eu

Bogdan and Van Broek Architects

Quai au Foin 55

1000 Brussels

T: 32 [0]2 60 90 065

www.bvbarchitects.com

The Office of Olson Sundberg Kundig Allen Architects

Architect: Olson Sundberg Kundig Allen Architects

159 Jackson St., Suite 600

Seattle, WA 98104

T:206.624.5670

www.oskarchitects.com

Structural Engineer: Monte Clarke Engineering

Jean Vollum Natural Capital Center

Architect: Holst Architecture

110 SE 8th

Portland, OR 97214

T: 503.233.9856

www.holstarc.com

Client: Ecotrust

General Contractor: Holst Architecture

Structural Engineer: KPFF Consulting Engineers

M/E/P Engineer: Interface Engineering, Inc.

The Smithsonian Tropical Research Institute

(STRI) Bocas del toro Laboratory

Architect: Kiss + Cathcart, Architects

44 Court St. Tower C

Brooklyn, NY 11201

T: 718.237.2786

F: 718.237.2025

Client: The Smithsonian Institute

IBN Institute For Forestry and Nature Research

Architect: Behnisch Architekten

163A Rotebuhl Istrasse

70197 Stuttgart, Germany

T: 49 711 607720

www.behnisch.com

Client: IBN Institute For Forestry and Nature Research

General Contractor: HITT Contracting, Inc.

Environmental Consultancy: Buro Happold

Structural Engineer: Buro Happold

M/E/P Engineer: Buro Happold

Lewis and Clark State Office Building

Architect: BNIM Architects (Berkebile Nelson

Immenschuh McDowell Architects)

106 West 14th Street Suite 200

Kansas City, Missouri 64105

T: 816.783.1500

www.bnim.com

Client: State of Missouri

General Contractor: Professional Contractors and

Engineers Inc.

Environmental Consultancy: ENSAR Group

Structural Engineer: Structural Engineering Assoc.

Electrical Engineer: Smith & Boucher

Directory

Green Door

Architect: Envision Design, PLLC

1211 Connecticut Avenue, NW

Suite 250

Washington, DC 20036

Tel: 202.775.9000

www.envisionsite.com

Environmental Service Building

Architect: Miller/ Hull Partnership, LLP

Polson Building

71 Columbia - Sixth Floor

Seattle, Washington 98104

T: 206.682.6837

www.millerhull.com

Bückeburg Gas & Water Company

Architect: Randall Stout Architects, Inc.

12964 Washington Blvd

Los Angeles, CA 90066

T: 310.827.6876

www.stoutarc.com

Client: Bükeburg Gas and Water

Greenpeace USA Headquarters

Architect: Envision Design, PLLC

1211 Connecticut Avenue, NW

Suite 250

Washington, DC 20036

Tel: 202.775.9000

www.envisionsite.com

Client: Greenpeace

General Contractor: Hitt Contracting, Inc.

Construction Manager: Mark G. Anderson Consultants

MEP Engineer: GHT, Ltd.

Structural Engineer: Rathgeber / Goss Associates

Sedgwick Rd

Architect: Olson Sundberg Kundig Allen Architects

159 Jackson St., Suite 600

Seattle, WA 98104

T:206.624.5670

www.oskarchitects.com

Client: Sedgwick Rd PR

The Gordon & Betty Moore Foundation

Architect: Gensler

1230 Avenue of the Americas Suite 1500

New York, New York

T: 212.492.1400

www.gensler.com

Client: Gordon Betty Moore Foundation

Aspect Communications

Architect: William McDonough + Partners

700 East Jefferson Street

Charlottesvile, VA 22902

T: 434.979.1111

www.mcdonough.com

Client: Aspect Communications, San Jose, California

Design Architects Building and Interior: Form4 Architect

General Contractor: DPR Construction

Structural Engineer: Middlebrook + Louie

M/E/P Engineer: Critchfield Mechanical, Inc + Frank Electric

Landscape Design Consultant: Susan Nelson - Warren Byrd

Landscape Architect of Record: April Philips Design Works

Carnegie Institute for Global Ecology

Client: Carnegie Institute, Stanford, CA

Architect: EHDD (Esherick, Homsey, Dodge, and Davis)

Architecture

Design Architects Building and Interior:

General Contractor:

Environmental Consultancy:

Structural Engineer: Rutherford & Chekene

Civil Engineer: BKF

M/E/P Engineer: Rumsey Engineers

Landscape Consultant: Lutsko Associates, Landscape

Directory

New York Times Building

Architect: Gensler

1230 Avenue of the Americas Suite 1500

New York, New York

T: 212.492.1400

www.gensler.com

Architect: Renzo Piano Building Workshop

Via Rbens 29, 16158 Genova, Italy

T: 39 010 61 711

www.rpbw.r.ui-pro.com

Architect: FXFOWLE Architects

22 W 19th Street

New York, NY 10011

T: 212.627.1700

www.fxfowle.com

Client: The New York Times Company

Architect: Renzo Piano Building Workshop/FXFOWLE Architects

Design Architects Building and Interior: Gensler

General Contractor: Turner Interiors

Structural Engineer: Thornton Tomasetti

Electrical Engineer: Flack + Kurtz

Mechanical Engineer: Flack + Kurtz

LEFT: White Rock operations building: Colin Jewall, photographers.

Glossary

ADAPTIVE REUSE: Renovation of an existing building or site that originally was intended for a different use.

AIR PLENUM: Any space used to convey air in a building, furnace or structure. The space above a suspended ceiling or under a raised floor can be used as an air plenum.

AIR POLLUTANT: Any natural or artificial substance capable of being airborne that could, in high enough concentration, harm man, other animals, vegetation or material.

ALTERNATIVE ENERGY: Energy from a source other than the conventional fossil-fuel sources of oil, natural gas and coal.

BIODIVERSITY: A large number and wide range of species of animals, plants, fungi and microorganisms.

BIOSWALES: Shallow vegetation filled landscape elements designed to remove silt and pollution from surface runoff water.

BLACKWATER: Water that contains animal, human, or food waste.

BREEAM: Acronym for the UK based Building Research Establishment Environmental Assessment Method. BREEAM is a comprehensive tool for analyzing and improving the environmental performance of buildings through design and operations.

BROWNFIELDS: Abandoned, idled or underused industrial and commercial facilities where expansion or redevelopment is complicated by real or perceived environmental contamination.

BRISE-SOLIEL: A solar shading device that controls the considerable heat gain created by large areas of glazing in modern buildings in order to make conditions more comfortable for the people inside.

BUILDING-RELATED ILLNESS: Diagnosable illness whose cause and symptoms can be directly attributed to a specific pollutant source within a building.

BUILDING ENVELOPE: The elements and materials that thermally enclose a building.

CERTIFIED: Buildings evaluated by a third party rating system. (See LEED and BREEAM.)

COMPOST: Process whereby organic wastes, including food wastes, paper and yard wastes, decompose naturally, resulting in a product rich in minerals and ideal for gardening and farming as a soil conditioner, mulch, resurfacing material or landfill cover.

COMMISSIONING: A process that occurs prior to building occupancy during which the performance of the building systems are checked and adjusted if necessary in order to ensure that they are operating as intended by the design.

CONSERVATION: Preserving and renewing, when possible, human and natural resources.

CISTERN: A receptacle for holding water or other liquid, especially a tank for catching and storing rainwater.

DAYLIGHTING: The use of natural light to supplement or replace artificial lighting.

DECONSTRUCTION: A process to carefully dismantle or remove useable materials from structures, as an alternative to demolition. It maximizes the recovery of valuable building materials for reuse and recycling and minimizes the amount of waste land-filled.

DISPLACEMENT VENTILATION: A method of space conditioning where conditioned air is supplied at or near the floor. Since the air is supplied at very low velocities, a cool layer of air collects in the occupied zone resulting in comfortable conditions for the occupants. Buoyant forces remove heat generated by occupants and equipment, as well as odors and pollutants, all of which stratify under the ceiling and are extracted from the space by return or exhaust fans. These systems are effective in improving indoor air quality as well as providing energy savings when compared to a conventional fully mixed system.

ECOLOGY: A branch of science concerned with the interrelationship of organisms and their environment.

ECOSYSTEM: An interconnected and symbiotic grouping of animals, plants, fungi and micro-organisms that sustains life through biological, geological and chemical activity.

EMBODIED ENERGY: Refers to both the energy required to construct, produce, and transport a product and the molecular energy that exists in a product's material content.

EMISSION: The release of any gas, particle, or vapor into the environment from a commercial, industrial, or residential source including smokestacks, chimneys, and motor vehicles.

ENVIRONMENTAL IMPACT: Any change to the environment, whether adverse or beneficial, wholly or partially resulting from human activity, industry or natural disasters.

ENVIRONMENTAL FOOTPRINT: For an industrial setting, this is a company's environmental impact determined by the amount of depletable raw materials and nonrenewable resources it consumes to make its products, and the quantity of wastes and emissions that are generated in the process. Traditionally, for a company to grow, the footprint had to get larger. Today, finding ways to reduce the environmental footprint is a priority for leading companies.

ENVIRONMENTAL RESTORATION: The act of repairing damage to a site caused by human activity, industry or natural disasters. The ideal environmental restoration, though rarely achieved, is to restore the site as closely as possible to its natural condition before it was disturbed.

EPA: The acronym for the U.S. Environmental Protection Agency, the Federal Government organization charged with setting and enforcing environmental regulations nationwide.

FLY ASH: A fine, glass-powder recovered from the gases of burning coal during the production of electricity. These micron- sized earth elements consist primarily of silica, alumina and iron. When mixed with lime and water the fly ash forms a cementitious compound with properties very similar to that of portland cement.

FLYWHEEL EFFECT: is the continuation of oscillations in an oscillator circuit after the control stimulus has been removed.

FORMALDEHYDE: It is a flammable, poisonous, colorless gas with a suffocating odor. Formaldehyde is prepared commercially by passing methanol vapor mixed with air over a catalyst, e.g., hot copper, to cause oxidation of the methanol; it is also prepared by the oxidation of natural gas. It has been identified as a carcinogen.

FSC: Acronym for the Forest Stewardship Council. FSC is a nonprofit organization that sets standards for forestry practices that are environmentally responsible, socially beneficial and economically viable.

GABION WALLS: Gabion Walls are generally analyzed as gravity retaining walls, that is, walls which use their own weight to resist the lateral earth pressures with the use of horizontal layers of welded wire mesh.

GEOTHERMAL HEAT PUMP: Geothermal heat pumps are also known as "geo-exchange" systems and "ground-source heat pumps." Geothermal systems use the natural heat storage capacity of the earth or ground water to provide energy efficient heating and cooling. These systems operate based on the stability of underground temperatures; the ground a few feet below surface has a very stable temperature throughout the year, typically somewhere in range of 50-85 °F (10-30 °C) depending upon location's annual climate.

Glossary

GRAYWATER: (Also greywater, or gray water) Wastewater from sinks, showers, kitchens, washers, etc. Unlike black water, gray water does not contain human waste. Typically gray water, after purification, is used for non-potable uses such as flushing, irrigation, etc.

GREEN: A term that is widely used to describe a building and site that is designed in an environmentally sensitive manner, i.e. with minimal impact to the environment.

GREEN BUILDING: A building that minimizes impact on the environment through resource (energy, water, etc.) conservation and contributes to the health of its occupants. Comfortable, aesthetically pleasing and healthful environments characterize green buildings.

GREEN DESIGN: is a term now widely used to describe buildings designed and constructed with minimal negative impact to the environment and with an emphasis on conservation of resources, energy efficiency, and healthful interior spaces.
Green design conforms to environmentally sound principles of building, material and energy use. Green is a term now widely used to describe buildings designed and constructed with minimal negative impact to the environment and with an emphasis on conservation of resources, energy efficiency, and healthful interior spaces.

GREEN ROOF: A roofing system that utilizes vegetation to absorb rain water and reduce heat reflection.

GREENSEAL: A non-profit organization that Green Seal provides science-based environmental certification standards.

HABITAT: The natural home of an animal or plant.

HEPA: A high efficiency particulate air or HEPA filter is a type of high-efficiency air filter.

HVAC: Acronym for Heating, Ventilation, Air conditioning.

INDOOR AIR QUALITY (IAQ): Indoor pollution sources that release gases or particles into the air are the primary cause of indoor air quality problems in buildings. Inadequate ventilation can increase indoor pollutant levels by not bringing in enough outdoor air to dilute emissions from indoor sources and by not carrying indoor air pollutants out of the home. High temperature and humidity levels can also increase concentrations of some pollutants.

INTEGRATED WASTE MANAGEMENT: The complementary use of a variety of practices to handle solid waste safely and effectively. Techniques include source reduction, recycling, composting, combustion and landfilling.

LEED™: LEED (Leadership in Energy and Environmental Design) is a self assessing system designed for rating new and existing commercial, institutional, and high-rise residential buildings. It evaluates environmental performance from a "whole building" perspective over a building's life cycle, providing a definitive standard for what constitutes a green building. (See LEED Rating System)

LEED™ Rating System: LEED is a point-based rating system developed by the US Green Building Council that evaluates the environmental performance from a "whole building" perspective over its life cycle, providing a definitive standard for what constitutes a green building according to six categories:

> Sustainable Sites
> Water Efficiency
> Energy and Atmosphere
> Material Resources
> Indoor Environmental Quality
> Innovation and Design Process

Buildings evaluated by LEED are rated as certified, silver, gold, or platinum.
There are a total of 69 LEED credits available in the six categories: 26 credits are required to attain the most basic level of LEED certification; 33 to 38 credits are needed for Silver; 39 to 51 credits for Gold; 52 to 69 credits for the Platinum rating.

LIFE CYCLE ASSESSMENT: The process of analyzing a product's entire life, from raw materials extraction through manufacturing, delivery, use, and disposal or reuse.

MILK PAINT: A non-toxic, fade-resistant paint made from milk protein (casein), clay, lime and earth pigments

ORGANIC COMPOUND: Vast array of substances typically characterized as principally carbon and hydrogen, but that may also contain oxygen, nitrogen and a variety of other elements as structural building blocks.

PERVIOUS: Pervious materials permit water to enter the ground by virtue of their porous nature or by large spaces in the material.

POST-CONSUMER RECYCLE CONTENT: A product composition that contains some percentage of material that has been reclaimed from the same or another end use at the end of its former, useful life.

POST-INDUSTRIAL RECYCLE CONTENT: Product composition that contains some percentage of manufacturing waste material that has been reclaimed from a process generating the same or a similar product. Also called pre-consumer recycle content.

PHOTOVOLTAIC ARRAY: A linked collection of photovoltaic modules, which are made of multiple interconnected solar cells. The cells convert solar energy into direct current electricity.

PVC: Polyvinyl chloride. Plastic, commonly referred to as vinyl, is one of the most hazardous consumer products ever created. PVC is dangerous to human health and environment throughout its entire lifecycle. PVC plastic releases dioxins, a group of the most potent synthetic chemicals ever tested, which can cause cancer and harm the immune and reproductive systems.

RAIN GARDEN: A rain garden is a planted area that is designed to absorb rainwater runoff from impervious urban areas like roofs, driveways, walkways. This reduces the amount of pollution reaching creeks and streams by allowing stormwater to soak into the ground instead of flowing into storm drains.

RECLAMATION: Restoration of materials found in the waste stream to a beneficial use that may be other than the original use.

RECLAIMED: Reclaimed building materials are those that have been salvaged from the waste stream and reused in their original form, with minimal reprocessing.

RECYCLING: Process by which materials that would otherwise become solid waste are collected, separated or processed and returned to the economic mainstream to be reused in the form of raw materials or finished goods.

RECYCLABLE CONTENT: Materials that can be recovered or diverted from the waste stream for recycling/reuse.

RENEWABLE RESOURCES: A resource that can be replenished at a rate equal to or greater than its rate of depletion; i.e., solar, wind, geothermal and biomass resources.

REUSE: Using an item more than once.

SANITARY WATER: Water discharged from sinks, showers, kitchens or other non-industrial operations, but not from commodes. Also referred to as "gray water." (See Graywater)

SICK BUILDING SYNDROME: A building whose occupants experience acute health and/or comfort affects that appear to be linked to time spent therein, but where no specific illness or cause can be identified. Complaints may be localized in a particular room or zone, or may spread throughout the building and may abate on leaving the building.

Glossary

STACK EFFECT: Flow of air resulting from warm air rising, creating a positive pressure area at the top of a building and negative pressure area at the bottom. This effect can overpower the mechanical system and disrupt building ventilation and air circulation.

STORMWATER: Stormwater is water that originates during precipitation or "storm" events. It may also be used to apply to water that originates with snowmelt or runoff water. Stormwater that does not soak into the ground becomes surface runoff (which carries potential contaminants that could contribute to water pollution), which either flows into surface waterways or is channeled into storm sewers.

SUSTAINABILITY: Sustainability refers to the concept that new development must meet the needs of the present without compromising those of the future. Sustainability is measured in three interdependent dimensions: the environment, economics, and society.

SUSTAINABLE DEVELOPMENT: An approach to progress that meets the needs of the present without compromising the ability of future generations to meet their needs.

SWALES: Swales (a.k.a. vegetated swales, grassed channel, dry swale, wet swale or biofilter) are constructed open-channel drainageways used to convey stormwater runoff. Vegetated swales are often used as an alternative to, or an enhancement of, traditional storm sewer pipes.

TOXIC: Any material or waste product that can produce injury and/or loss of life if inhaled, swallowed, or absorbed through the skin.

THERMAL MASS: A mass (often stone, concrete, or brick) used to store heat and reduce temperature fluctuation in a space, by releasing heat slowly over time.

U.S. GREEN BUILDING COUNCIL (USGBC): Acronym for a national organization, whose mission is to accelerate the adoption of green building practices, technologies, policies, and standards. USGBC established the LEED Certification guidelines.

UNDER-FLOOR AIR DISTRIBUTION SYSTEM: Under-floor heating is a form of central heating which utilizes heat conduction and radiant heat for indoor climate control, rather than forced air heating which relies on convection.

VENTILATION: Process by which outside air is conveyed to an indoor space.

VOLATILE ORGANIC COMPOUND (VOC): Materials that evaporate, either through use or during storage, from many household and industrial products made with organic chemicals. In sufficient quantities, VOCs are suspected of causing or exacerbating acute and chronic illnesses.

WASTEWATER: The used water from a home, community, farm, or industry that contains dissolved or suspended matter.

WATER-SOURCE HEAT PUMP: Heat pump that uses wells or heat exchangers to transfer heat from water to the inside of a building.

WATERLESS URINAL: Urinal with no water line. Most designs use a specialized material that allows fluid to drain one-way into the sewer system.

WETLAND: An area that is saturated by surface or ground water with vegetation adapted for life under those soil conditions, as swamps, bogs, fens, marshes, and estuaries.

SOURCES:

1: http://www.epa.gov/OCEPAterms/aterms.html
2: http://antron.dupont.com/content/resources/green_glossary
3:http://www.eia.doe.gov/cneaf/solar.renewables/page/rea_data/gl.ht
ml
4: http://lightingdesignlab.com/library/glossary.htm
5. Big & Green: Toward Sustainable Architecture in the 21st Century,
published in 2002 by Princeton Architectural Press7.
http://www.montgomeryschoolsmd.org Green Glossary by Tom
Paxton